The Blair Necessities

The Blair Necessities

*The Tony Blair
Book of Quotations*

IAIN DALE

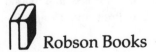

Robson Books

First published in Great Britain in 1997 by Robson Books Ltd, Bolsover House, 5–6 Clipstone Street, London W1P 8LE

The author is grateful for permission to reprint Fleur Adcock's poem and articles written by Matthew Parris.

British Library Cataloguing in Publication Data
A catalogue record for this title is available from the British Library

ISBN 1 86105 139 5

Set in Palatino in North Wales by Derek Doyle & Associates, Mold, Flintshire. Printed and bound in Great Britain by Creative Print and Design Wales, Ebbw Vale.

This book is dedicated to my parents,
Jane and Garry Dale

'The opportunity to serve – that is all we ask.'

Last public words of Rt Hon John Smith MP, 11 May 1994

He was the youngest Prime Minister of the century, at the peak of his energy and ability, filled with wonder at his success ... and with a terrific sense of what he might yet achieve.

Ben Pimlott on Harold Wilson's win in 1964

Can it be that I was unfair
To Tony Blair?

His teeth, after all, are beyond compare;
But does he take too much care
Over his hair?

If he were to ask me out for a meal,
How would I feel?
Would I grovel and kneel,
Aflame with atavistic socialist zeal?
No, I'm sorry, he doesn't appeal:
he's not quite real.

In the House he sounds sincere,
But over a candlelit table, I fear,
His accents wouldn't ring sweetly in my ear.
Oh dear.

I'd love to see him in Number Ten,
But he doesn't match my taste in men.

by Fleur Adcock

Contents

Foreword

Just who is Tony Blair? The most able Labour leader since Attlee, or 'Phoney Tony'? Everyone has a view, but the truth is that nobody knows. As Britain's youngest Prime Minister this century he carries the hopes of millions of people upon his shoulders. The Blair era has begun.

As with all good ideas, the idea for this book came about totally by accident. Having compiled one book of quotations (*As I Said to Denis . . . The Margaret Thatcher Book of Quotations*) I had not really contemplated doing another one. However, while discussing a different book with my publishers at Robson Books someone came up with the idea of *The Blair Necessities*. I can't even remember if it was me.

And so a book was born. This book seeks neither to praise Blair or denigrate him. All it tries to do is to help the reader understand both the man and his beliefs. It attempts to plot the development of his political thinking and character as well as point out some of the inconsistencies which have come to light in a political career spanning fifteen years. Policy flip-flops are inevitable in any political career and no one should be surprised that Tony Blair has performed quite a number over the last few years. The simple truth is that had he not done so, he would not be Prime Minister today.

I have never voted Labour. Perhaps not surprising for one who hails from God's own county of Essex. I was a teenager in the late 1970s and came to associate Labour with strikes, trade union militancy and CND. My early adult years were spent advocating Thatcherite economic and foreign policies. The last few years have been spent observing politics from the outside, becoming increasingly disillusioned with the way the Conservative government lost its direction and slightly appalled at the conduct and quality of our elected representatives.

So why is it that an unreconstructed Thatcherite like me finds Tony Blair such a source of fascination? Perhaps because there are many parallels to be drawn between Blair and Thatcher. They both possess outstanding leadership qualities together with an unusual ability to develop populist policies which have a wide appeal electorally. They both took their respective Parties by the scruff of the neck and administered a much needed dose of political realism.

My fascination with Tony Blair is perhaps also more to do with the new political landscape and the fact that politics have become interesting again. How will Blair cope with the Old Labour element in his Party and among his 418 Members of Parliament? How will he cope with the spending demands which his Party will make on him? Will he handle the European question any better than his predecessor? We don't know the answers to these questions yet, but this book will hopefully help the reader form a judgement on Blair's likelihood of success.

The first quote in this book comes from the late John Smith. I wonder if I am alone in feeling that both John Smith and Neil Kinnock have too soon been consigned to history by New Labour. In all Tony Blair's many speeches following his land-slide victory, not once did he pay significant tribute to his imme-diate predecessor beyond a cursory mention. A simple 'This one's for you, John' might have been nice. But then, politics is about the present. The past is about history.

Similarly, without Neil Kinnock's Party reforms, it would not have been possible for someone like Tony Blair to become leader. Few of us will forget the sight of Neil Kinnock watching events on the night of 1 May, not as a senior figure in the Labour Party sharing in its triumph by the side of its new leader, but as a guest of Mr Jeremy Paxman in a BBC TV studio. Different time, different place. It is anyone's guess how often Neil Kinnock must have thought, 'That could have been me.'

Having compiled this book in a relatively short period of time it is even more incumbent on me than usual to thank those who have both helped me complete the task, and shown patience and understanding for the time I have spent on the book, when perhaps I should have been doing other things.

Firstly, thanks are due to Jeremy Robson and Kate Mills at Robson Books for their confidence in me and their valued advice. Secondly, I am indebted to my colleagues at Politico's Bookstore, who have suffered from overwork and an impatient Managing Director. John Simmons has been a tower of strength to me personally and professionally and deserves full credit for thinking up the titles of both this and my previous book. Thanks also to Nick Ostler, Dean Williams, Andrea Frost and Enid Simmons.

I would like to thank numerous Labour Party staff and supporters for their co-operation and helpfulness during my research. In addition thanks are due to the Conservative Research Department for their co-operation. In particular I am also indebted to Malcolm Gooderham for his time and efforts in providing me with research and information.

I take full responsibility for any errors. Where possible each quote is fully sourced. A full bibliography of reference sources is included at the end of the book.

Having been involved in politics one way or another for nearly twenty years, as a student, parliamentary researcher, journalist, lobbyist and now political bookshop owner, I would like to take this opportunity to mention and thank a few people who have, over time, helped me, taught me, argued with me, fought me and worked with me. They include Audrey Barker, Graham Brady, Steve Bramall, Michael Carttiss, Michael Clark, Peter Cropper, Bob Crossan, David Davis, Richard Evans, Nick Finney, Judy Fletcher, Daniel Forrester, Conal Gregory, Sir Alan Haselhurst, Ernie and Joan Horth, Robert Key, Arthur and Norrie Kemp, Andrew MacKinlay, Roger Moate, Patrick

Nicholls, Mike Norris, Steve Norris, John and Jill Powley, Tim
Quint, Phyllis Reeve, Roger Rosewell, Mark Seddon, Deborah
and Mike Slattery, Patrick and Kathleen Thompson, and Gordon
Turner.

There are many Labour Party supporters with whom I have
enjoyed friendly argument and debate over the years – this one's
for them.

Iain Dale
June 1997

Part One

THE MEANING OF LIFE

Early Years and Background

He was the most difficult boy I ever had to deal with.
A former teacher at Fettes School, Mail on Sunday, *22 June 1994*

*

He was unforgettable. He was one of those people whose presence in the room was always noticeable. At times a pain in the neck, but fundamentally great fun to have around. He was intensely argumentative and every school rule was questioned. He could uphold his side of the debate about the rights and wrongs of everything better than any boy in the school. I think I would have guessed that he would become a top barrister in his time, but not that he would go into the Labour Party.
Blair's Housemaster, Eric Anderson, Sunday Times, *19 July 1992*

*

Tony was something of an expert at testing the rules to the limit ... He was the sort of boy that you were always

struggling with to have his hair cut.
Eric Anderson, Blair's English teacher, BBC TV, 21 November 1988

*

He thought for himself which ... was something that was rather frowned upon. He was no respecter of authority, which in its own way was admired by all the other boys in the class. His hair was always a bit too long, but never outrageously so, and he would look scruffy. He would sit with either shoulders slouched or his head cocked back. He really knew how to show he was pissed off with the masters without actually saying so.
Classmate Alastair Campbell, quoted in Tony Blair – The Modernizer *by Jon Sopel*

*

We had a perfectly good, average, middle-class standard of living.

*

We are a very close-knit family. But it was as though all the security that as a youngster you take for granted and think will be there for ever had been shattered in an instant. On an emotional level, I was suddenly made aware that nothing is permanent. You think as a child your parents are indestructible; that they will live for ever. But there was my father, unable to speak, having been lucky to survive.
On his father's stroke

*

One of the formative events of my life.
On his father's stroke, Evening Standard, *16 November 1993*

*

After his illness, my father transferred his ambitions onto his kids. It imposed a certain discipline. I felt I couldn't let him down.
Interview in the Sunday Times, *17 July 1994*

*

He made particularly good toast.
Michael Gascoigne (Blair was his fag at Fettes School)

*

Reading from top to bottom, the long hair with the rather severe fringe – a slightly medieval look about him, a sort of Three Musketeers thing – a T-shirt that can only be described as 'hoop-necked' and possibly even 'trumpet-sleeved', which revealed a large acreage of rippling bare torso, and beyond that the obligatory purple loons, topped off with the Cuban-heeled cowboy boots.
Mark Ellen on the appearance of Tony Blair as lead singer in the rock band Ugly Rumours, *BBC TV, 10 June 1994*

*

I could never stand the Oxford intellectual establishment – they seemed to have a poker up their backsides.
Interview in the Sunday Times, *17 July 1994*

*

I attended the births of Euan and Kathryn, and only missed the arrival of Nicholas because he was early . . . You feel pretty useless. But I'm pleased I was there. It's good for your part-

ner, I think, and you're humbled by what she goes through.
Evening Standard, *16 November 1993*

*

I have never found my educational background a problem with ordinary voters. I have only ever found it a problem with middle-class journalists.
Interview in the Independent, *2 July 1994*

*

He bowled me over with his enthusiasm.
Derry (later Lord) Irvine, on meeting the young lawyer Blair

Family Values

Derry (Irvine) took us out to lunch and he disappeared after a time and I remember we were still there at dinner-time, so something must have happened along the way.
On his first 'date' with Cherie, Desert Island Discs, *23 November 1996*

*

The first time I met Cherie I thought she was incredibly bright – a bit of a swot . . . I was attracted to her because of her looks, of course, but also because she was so different . . . She's a one-off, totally her own person. She's a friend, someone I respect as well as love.
Daily Mirror, *8 March 1997*

*

I had my last cigarette at 1.45pm and we married at two. It was my wife's idea, one of the terms of the contract, and I'm glad to say I still think I made the right bargain.
Evening Standard, *16 November 1993*

*

I'm quite a private person and want to protect our children. When Tony takes them to school the other kids are always

7

saying, 'We saw you on the telly last night.' I don't want my children growing up thinking that they're special, just because of what their daddy does.

Cherie Booth, New Woman, *May 1994*

*

If I didn't actually believe in what Tony was doing it would be far more difficult to cope. But I'm very proud of him. I think that he's got a lot to offer and I really want him to succeed. The fact that Tony's fairly famous and I'm not doesn't bother me at all. I'm well paid and highly regarded in my own field.

Cherie Booth, New Woman, *May 1994*

*

I started life as the daughter of someone, now I am the wife of someone and I'll probably end up as the mother of someone.

Cherie Booth, Today, *22 July 1994*

*

When I'm home, I'm home. I don't sit here having great political thoughts. While it's obviously harder now to make time for the family I do still try very hard.

Yes Magazine, *27 April 1997*

*

She's a private person who's reluctantly learning to cope with the media interest in her. I admire the way she's been prepared to go out and face it.

Daily Mirror, *8 March 1997*

*

I can probably cook most things if I put my mind to it, but not very well.
Yes Magazine, *27 April 1997*

*

When someone very close to you dies, you are brought up short with the nature of life, and the fact that if you want to do certain things, you had better get on and do them.
On the effect of his mother's death, Desert Island Discs, *23 November 1996*

*

I wish that my children could have known my mother.
Daily Mirror, *8 March 1997*

*

One wall of the dining room is lined with Cherie's law books, the other wall with erotic nude paintings. I counted a total of eleven nipples on display.
Nigel Nelson, Yes Magazine, *27 April 1997*

*

After the great 'smack' debate (the one about violence not drugs) Tony Blair admitted that he'd smacked his children when little. He did say he was sorry, however. Not half as sorry as they were, I bet.
From The Very Bloody History of Britain 2, *entry for June 1996*

*

He offered to join. Although I have to say that I think it was blood being thicker than water.
On his father Leo's decision to join the Labour Party after a lifetime as a Conservative, Desert Island Discs, *23 November 1996*

Values

I am a socialist not through reading a textbook that has caught my intellectual fancy, nor through unthinking tradition, but because I believe that, at its best, socialism corresponds most closely to an existence that is both rational and moral. It stands for co-operation, not confrontation; for fellowship, not fear. It stands for equality, not because it wants people to be the same but because only through equality in our economic circumstances can our individuality develop properly. British democracy rests ultimately on the shared perception by all the people that they participate in the benefits of the common weal.

Maiden speech in the House of Commons, 6 July 1983

*

I went through all the bit about reading Trotsky and attempting a Marxist analysis. But it never went very deep, and there was always the self-evident wrongness of what was happening in Eastern Europe.

Sunday Telegraph, *18 March 1990*

*

10

The real objection to equality is not reason but prejudice.
Hansard, 21 February 1994

*

Labour's vision is of a Britain that is not just a collection of individuals but a society where a decent community backs up the efforts of the individuals within it. That change can't come through market forces. It needs active government, local and national.
Interview in the Sunday Mirror, *8 May 1994*

*

The great thing is to stick by what we think and believe.
Interview in The Times, *6 July 1994*

*

If someone's making the choice to bring up a child as a single parent, I'm very surprised at that . . . If they do, I personally don't agree with them in doing that . . . Is it better that our kids are brought up with two parents? The answer plainly is yes.
Interview with Brian Walden, 24 July 1994

*

Our outdated and decrepit constitution that now combines the worst features of the centralizing tendency of government with unaccountable quangos and cartels taking over local services. A new settlement between citizen and society requires radical reform of our constitution and such reforms should be pursued by a Labour government.
Article in Fabian Pamphlet 565, *July 1994*

*

I feel a perfectly normal person. I look at politicians who are older than me and I wonder when was the last time they had their own thoughts to themselves in their own way without feeling they had to programme their thoughts to get across a message.
The Times, *1 October 1994*

*

The art of leadership is saying no, not yes. It is very easy to say yes.
Mail on Sunday, *2 October 1994*

*

Responsibility is a value shared. If it doesn't apply to everyone it ends up applying to no one.
Speech to Labour Party Conference, 4 October 1994

*

A young country that wants to be a strong country cannot be morally neutral about the family.
Speech to the Labour Party Conference, 3 October 1995

*

My view of Christian values led me to oppose what I perceived to be a narrow view of self-interest that Conservatism – particularly in its modern, more right wing form – represents. Every human being is self-interested. But Tories, I think, have too selfish a definition of that self-interest. They fail to look beyond to the community and the

individual's relationship with the community.
Sunday Telegraph, *7 April 1996*

*

One Britain. That is the patriotism for the future. Where your child in distress is my child; your parent ill and in pain is my parent; your friend unemployed or helpless, my friend; your neighbour, my neighbour.
Speech to the Labour Party Conference, 3 October 1996

*

It is no good waving the fabric of our flag when you have spent the last sixteen years tearing apart the fabric of our nation. Tearing apart the bonds which tie communities together and make us a United Kingdom.
Ibid.

*

Obviously some people will interpret this in a way which is harsh and unpleasant but I think the basic principle here is to say: yes it is right to be intolerant of people homeless on the streets.
Big Issue, *January 1997*

*

We have reached the limit of the public's willingness simply to fund an unreformed welfare system through ever higher taxation and spending.
Hansard, *15 May 1997*

The Radical Tony Blair

Labour does need a bold and radical identity. It does need to be clear as to what it stands for, as well as what it is against. It does require vision. No left of centre party has ever won a clear majority to govern without it.

Fabian Review, *September/October 1993*

*

New Labour moves beyond the solutions of old left and new right. We are a radical party.

Renewal, *October 1995*

*

I believe we have broken through the traditional barriers of left and right; that we are developing a new and radical economic approach for the left and the centre.

Speech in Tokyo, 5 January 1996

*

The solutions of neither the old left nor the new right will do.

We need a new radical centre in modern politics that can answer this competitive challenge whilst enhancing social stability and cohesion.
Speech in New York, 11 February 1996

*

I am a radical. I believe the centre can be fertile ground for radical politics ... A modern party, to be successful in the modern world, must be in the centre, speaking for the mainstream majority, addressing their concerns. Only such a party can govern well.
Speech in New York, 11 April 1996

*

Radical on the economy. Radical on welfare. Radical on education. Old baggage discarded. New thinking required.
Speech in Swansea, 10 May 1996

*

It is New Labour that is the One Nation party today. New Labour, a party of One Nation Radicals.
Ibid.

*

If you look at Labour's policies, no one can conceivably say that's a cautious programme. It's a very radical programme.
New Statesman, *5 July 1996*

*

I am of the Centre-Left and I want the Left to be part of this project. I want the Left to realize that if we win this election, we will have done so without ceding any ground that cannot be recovered. I'm going to be a lot more radical in government than people think.

Observer, *27 April 1997*

New Labour – New Morality

Christianity is a very tough religion. It may not always be practised as such. But it is. It places a duty, an imperative on us to reach our better self and to care about creating a better community to live in.
In Reclaiming the Ground

*

I can't stand politicians who go on about religion.
Article in Vanity Fair, *March 1995*

*

We cannot live in a moral vacuum. If we do not learn and then teach the value of what is right and what is wrong, then the result is simple moral chaos which engulfs us all.
Guardian, *20 February 1993*

*

It is largely from family discipline that social discipline and a sense of responsibility is learnt. A modern notion of society –

17

where rights and responsibilities go together – requires
responsibility to be nurtured. Out of a family from the sense
of community. The family is the starting place.
25 June 1993

*

Take the family, the Right lays claim to being the guardian of
family values. The Left, in the past, was sometimes perceived
as treating the issues as irrelevant or even, in extreme cases,
as politically incorrect. The truth is that, of course, families
matter and family breakdown is an important underlying
cause of delinquent behaviour. Parental guidance is vital. But
what is the Right's answer to this? To stop benefits, so that the
children should suffer even more? That would not just be
wrong, but counter-productive.
Speech in Richmond, 15 October 1993

*

It's dangerous for politicians to get sucked into private morality and preach to people ... Politicians are not saints and I
don't pretend to be – and nobody else should pretend to be.
Sunday Mirror, *10 July 1994*

*

For the first time in a generation, it is the right-wing that
appears lost and disillusioned. No longer believing in their
own language, they turn to ours. Some are trying out
'community'. 'Partnership'. Even 'fairness'. Some are now
talking of Civic Conservatism. A contradiction in terms.
Speech to Labour Party Conference, 4 October 1994

*

We understand both the need for a new moral purpose in politics and have the individual, family and social values capable of sustaining it.
Speech to NewsCorp, 17 July 1995

*

Our challenge to be a young country is not just economic. It is a social and moral challenge.
Speech to Labour Party Conference, 3 October 1995

*

A young country that wants to be a strong country cannot be morally neutral about the family.
Ibid.

*

The left can fashion a new moral purpose for the nation which combines individual and social responsibility ... it has the moral authority to enforce the rules because it sets them within an active and strong community.
Renewal, *October 1995*

*

We need a new social morality.
Speech in Cape Town, 14 October 1996

*

A modern civic society, what I have called the Decent Society, is a necessary part of our western nations continuing to make

progress . . . Such a society cannot be created unless it is based on certain values, a social morality fit and right for today's world.
Ibid.

*

Most children who are bad are made bad, not born bad. And we, the parents and the society we create, are what make them.
Ibid.

*

Let the social morality be based on reason, not bigotry. But let us not delude ourselves that we can build a better society fit for our children to grow up in, without making a moral judgement about the nature of that society.
Ibid.

*

I don't want to switch the clock back, and I don't want to engage in some sort of Victorian hypocrisy about sex, or homophobia or you know women being confined to the kitchen, we need a social morality for today's world.
BBC Radio, 14 October 1996

Democracy

The central question of modern democratic politics is how to provide security during revolutionary change. That is what people look for from the governments they elect. And I don't just mean economic security. They want social stability too.

Speech in Australia, 17 July 1995

*

Our position is clear. We will be advocating a Scottish Parliament with tax varying powers.

Interview in the New Statesman, 5 July 1996

*

I would rather young people voted Tory or Liberal Democrat or Nationalist or Green rather than that they didn't vote at all.

Guardian, 13 July 1996

*

I'm not persuaded of the case for PR.

Interview in the New Statesman, 5 July 1996

*

I think the funding of the political parties should be open . . . people should know where the sources of money come from.
BBC TV, 12 January 1997

*

Let me tell you I would expect Ministers in a Government I lead to resign if they lie to Parliament. I would expect Ministers to pay their own legal fees if they get into personal difficulty. I would not allow foreign businessmen to bankroll a political party while not even paying any taxes in this country. And I would expect to know if a Member of Parliament in the Labour Party asked a Parliamentary Question they did so out of duty to their constituents not because £1,000 has been sent to their home address.
On how he would react to sleaze in a Labour administration

*

This is not a party political game or even a serious debate about serious run-of-the-mill issues. It is about life and death for people here.
Speaking in Belfast about the Northern Ireland peace process, 16 May 1997

*

Unionists have nothing to fear from a New Labour government. A political settlement is not a slippery slope to a united Ireland. The Government will not be persuaders for unity.
Ibid.

*

The settlement train is leaving. I want you on that train. But it is leaving anyway and I will not allow it to wait for you.
Directed at Sinn Fein, ibid.

Part Two

THE ECONOMY, STUPID!

Trade Unions

The issue is not whether elections are good or bad, but whether it is right for the state to intervene and to dictate to trade unions how they should conduct their affairs . . . [It is] an extraordinary proposition that it is the proper role of government to interfere in the due process of a voluntary organization.

Hansard, *8 November 1983, debating the Trade Union Bill*

*

It is a disgrace that we should be debating today the taking away of fundamental freedoms for which British trade unionists have fought for a long time. Having fought long and hard for them, they will not give them up lightly. We shall oppose the Bill, which is a scandalous and undemocratic measure against the trade union movement for partisan reasons.

Ibid.

*

In an article for the *New Statesman* in February 1980 Blair wrote indignantly that Jim Prior's proposals to outlaw secondary picketing were a 'concerted attempt to destroy the effectiveness of industrial action'. The following year, in the same magazine, he complained that 'the squeeze on the closed shop is to be made tighter still'. If Norman Tebbit's employment bill was passed, he warned, 'trade union law will be pushed back into the nineteenth century'.

Francis Wheen for Esquire, *quoting* New Statesman, *February 1990*

*

It's an absurd distortion to suggest there are groups of workers all over the place waiting to launch themselves into industrial action.

The Times, *8 October 1990*

*

The trade unions, for instance, are a classic example of institutions founded on a principle that is manifestly correct, stemming from a very strong belief in social justice; but let us be clear about it, by the end of the seventies the public perception of trade unions was not that they were assisting the individual, they were there as vested interests and therefore you had to transform that.

Guardian, *29 June 1991*

*

People should have the entitlement to strike . . . It should be exercised because it is a right.

BBC TV, *26 June 1994*

*

I have heard people saying a Labour Government should repeal all the Tory trade union laws. Now, there is not a single person in this country who believes that we shall actually do it. No one believes strike ballots should be abandoned. So

why do we say it? We shouldn't and I won't.
Speech to the Labour Party Conference, 4 October 1994

*

People accuse me of distancing the Labour Party from the unions. It's not distance I want but clarity.
Speech to TUC Conference, 12 September 1995

*

It is surely time to shift the emphasis in corporate ethos towards a vision of a company as a community of partnership in which each employee has a stake, and where a company's responsibilities are more clearly delineated.
Speech in Singapore, 8 January 1996

*

There is no going back on the Thatcherite trade union reforms.
Daily Telegraph, *January 1996*

*

There was and is no secret plan to 'dump' the unions.
LIFFE Lecture, 16 September 1996

*

The policy-making in the Labour Party is completely different and of course the trade unions now have no special position in relation to the selection of Members of Parliament . . . it

must be absolutely clear to the British people that we are a
political arm of no one other than the British people themselves.
BBC Radio, 4 October 1996

*

Trade unions are an important part of our democracy. I
support trade unions. I don't believe that trade unions should
be shut out in the cold and not listened to, as the Tories do.
Newsweek, *October 1996*

*

Modern trade unionism doesn't want to re-fight the battles
over secondary pickets and all the rest of it.
BBC Radio, 21 January 1997

*

We have revolutionized our relations with the trade unions,
to make clear that we offer fairness, not favours in government.
Daily Telegraph, *18 March 1997*

*

The unions will get fairness but no favours from us and
anyone who thinks we have created today's Labour Party
only to hand it over to the unions or anyone else does not
know me and has not been listening to a word I have said
these past three years. This is a party that will govern for all
the people, the whole country – and no single interest group
within it.
Labour Election Press Conference, 25 March 1997

Stakeholding

In a Stakeholder Economy, there will be a proper relationship of trust between business and Government ... The same relationship of trust and partnership applies within a firm. The successful companies are the ones which invest, treat their employees fairly and value them as a resource not merely of production but of creative innovation ... A shared responsibility for success, a sense of mutual purpose ... Close and long-term relationships are established with key suppliers ... In decision-making managers keep a firm eye on the future development of the business, as well as this week's or this year's bottom line.

Speech to British Retail Consortium, 14 February 1996

*

There is no future for a strong modern economy unless we treat citizens as stakeholders.

The Times, *18 September 1995*

*

The economics of the centre and centre-left today should be geared to the creation of the Stakeholder Economy which involves all our people. Not a privileged few or even a better off 30% or 40% or 50%. It is surely time to shift the emphasis in corporate ethos towards a vision of a company as a community of partnership in which each employee has a stake and where a company's responsibilities are more clearly delineated.

Speech in Singapore, 8 January 1996

*

The Stakeholder Economy has a Stakeholder Welfare System. By that I mean that the system will only flourish in its aims of promoting security and opportunity across the life-cycle if it holds the commitment of the whole population, rich and poor. This requires that everyone has a stake.

Ibid.

*

Stakeholders in a modern economy will today, more frequently than ever before, be self-employed or small businesses. We should encourage this, diversify the range of help and advice for those wanting to start out on their own.

Ibid.

*

The Conservatives are saying for example that the Stakeholder Economy is all about giving power back to the trade unions which is a nonsense.

BBC TV, 14 January 1996

*

Business leaders recognize that what New Labour is saying fits exactly with current thinking in industry. Some of our

great companies are stakeholder firms – John Lewis, Rover, M
& S, BP. Business advisers like John Kay, and Charles Handy
say that competitiveness and success come from a stakeholder approach.

Speech in Derby, 18 January 1996

*

Empowering the individual in a strong and cohesive society
is what the Stakeholder Economy is about.

Speech to Nottingham Chamber of Commerce, 19 January 1996

*

Stakeholding is not just about changing the relationship of a
company with its workforce and its customers . . . The whole
concept of stakeholding as developed by many people in
business is saying look, we get better value for our shareholders if we behave in this way. But it is not something that
I envisage a government being able to come through and
enforce.

Financial Times, *16 January 1997*

New Labour New Business

We are examining ways in which changes in the tax regime, or in take-over regulations, might sensibly be modified to encourage a long-term mentality in the City.
Mais Lecture, 22 May 1995

*

I think if this country is going to succeed its workforce has got to have an entirely different attitude, it has to have something of the spirit of the entrepreneur.
BBC Radio, 13 November 1995

*

Britain needs successful people in business who can become rich by their success, through the money they earn.
Speech to CBI Conference, 13 November 1995

*

It is surely time to shift the emphasis in corporate ethos towards a vision of a company as a community of partnership

in which each employee has a stake, and where a company's responsibilities are more clearly delineated.
Speech in Singapore, 8 January 1996

*

The sensible company today realizes that it's not just about its shareholders, important though they are, it is also about its employees, it's also about the community in which it operates and it is important that we have a notion of responsibility amongst the company. It's not something driven through by legislation, but something that we encourage.
BBC TV, 14 January 1996

*

I am not interested in red tape, regulation for the sake of regulation or adding needless burdens to business costs.
Speech to British Retail Consortium, 14 February 1996

*

A Labour government will encourage people to become wealthy if they do so by hard work, taking risks and above all creating jobs. There are a number of steps we can take – business schools could run entrepreneur courses for mature students with experience in manufacturing as they do in the United States.
Speech at Cranfield, 11 June 1996

*

I don't think that government is qualified to pick winners or to create entrepreneurs.
Speech in Bonn, 18 June 1996

*

We will introduce a requirement on large companies to publish their payment practices and for government departments and public agencies to pay their bills within thirty days.
Speech in Birmingham, 3 July 1996

*

New Labour is pro-business, pro-enterprise, and we believe there is nothing inconsistent between that and a decent and just society.
Financial Times, *16 January 1997*

*

I want entrepreneurs to stay here and succeed . . . I want more people to become millionaires through enterprise.
Daily Telegraph, *18 February 1997*

*

We want to see successful, profit making companies.
Speech to Guardian/*Nexus Conference, 1 March 1997*

*

I don't want to knock people down who have done well. If people go out and make a lot of money by the strength of their own endeavours that's great . . . if someone goes out and starts their own business and makes a success of it, that's great. We need more of that in Britain.
GMTV, 18 March 1997

Tough on Inflation, Tough on Public Spending

Gordon Brown and I have committed the Labour Party to follow a clear target for inflation.
Speech to CBI Conference, 13 November 1995

*

Government must keep its own borrowing on a sustainable course. We are committed to follow the golden rule of borrowing only for investment over the cycle, and will stabilize the debt to GDP ratio at a stable, prudent level.
Ibid.

*

We will have an explicit target for low and stable inflation as well as a medium-term objective of raising the economy's productive potential.
Ibid.

*

A business plan is virtually useless if you cannot plan ahead on the basis of stable prices. That is why Labour will take no

risk with inflation and will reject short-term quick-fix solutions.
Ibid.

*

A high spend economy is not a high success economy.
Speech in Swansea, 10 May 1996

*

We will be fierce in containing public spending. Governments in most European countries have to reduce budget deficits irrespective of the Maastricht criteria. The question is not whether but how.
Speech in Bonn, 18 June 1996

*

A New Labour government will have an explicit target for low and stable inflation and adhere to strict rules on borrowing and spending.
LIFFE Lecture, 16 September 1996

*

World interest rates and inflation rates are low. In Britain, under Labour we will keep them this way.
Speech to Labour Party Conference, 3 October 1996

*

Our priorities should be to re-order public spending so that we're spending less on welfare, and more on areas like education.
Newsweek, 7 October 1996

*

If you mess up the finances of the country, it's ordinary
people that end up paying.
Ibid.

*

Go-it-alone inflation or spending policies will be mercilessly
and immediately punished by capital markets that can over-
whelm a nation's currency.
Speech in Cape Town, 14 October 1996

*

We cannot compromise the need for macro-economic stability.
Low inflation and low interest rates combine to encourage
investment that is the only route to lasting prosperity.
Guardian, *23 November 1996*

*

We have set tougher rules for government borrowing than the
Conservatives have.
BBC Radio, 19 December 1996

*

The days when government shovelled out more money are
just not going to happen any more.
Big Issue, *January 1997*

*

There are no hidden spending increases, there are no spending commitments that are not made absolutely clear here, and

where they are made they are entirely properly costed and
funded.
Leading Britain into the Future, Press Conference, 8 January 1997

*

We will keep to the spending plans already laid down for the
next two years.
Daily Telegraph, *3 February 1997*

*

Tax is a problem if spending is a problem.
BBC TV, 12 February 1997

Blair Economics

The mild tinkering with the economy proposed by the Social Democrats nowhere near measures up to the problem. A massive reconstruction of industry is needed ... the resources required to reconstruct manufacturing industry call for enormous state guidance and intervention.

1982

*

The Tories say there is no money to create new jobs. But they spend billions of pounds on dangerous nuclear weapons. They spend billions on keeping people on the dole. They encourage the rich to invest billions abroad each year. This isn't sense, it's insanity!

Tony Blair's Election Address leaflet, June 1983

*

We will protect British industry against unfair foreign competition.

Ibid.

*

There is nothing odd about subsidizing an industry. To proceed in such a way is sensible.
Hansard, *15 November 1983*

*

The notion that we have created a generation of stock market investors is fatuous. All that has been shown is that if something is given away, it will be gratefully received. Of course, if Labour promises to take the gift back, it will not excite popularity among the beneficiaries. None of this means that privatization is right, or means that public ownership is wrong.
The Times, *29 September 1987*

*

There is now a mood of hard-headed enquiry about the City on which Labour must build. This goes much further than 'City scandals' – they are the gossip of the matter. More vital is to attack the system at its fundamentals; then to propose a radical and constructive alternative.
After the Stock Market Crash, Guardian, *23 October 1987*

*

Several myths, sedulously cultivated by the government and its supporters over three terms of office, died a violent death. The first and most significant is the rationality of the market, the economic lynch pin of Mrs Thatcher's big idea, the invisible power supposed to be working to our common good.
Ibid.

*

The market collapsed: its guardians, the City whizz-kids with salaries only fractionally less than their greed, now seem not just morally dubious, but incompetent. They failed miserably, proving themselves utterly unfit to have such power.
Ibid.

*

Politically, the fall-out from the events of the last two weeks will be immense. There will be few politicians standing for election next time on a platform advocating 'free markets'.
News on Sunday, *1 November 1987*

*

It is high time we reasserted the value of those who work to produce or to serve, in manufacturing and in services. Their future and ours is surely more important than the activities of those who chase paper profits in the casino economy of the markets.
Ibid.

*

I have not accepted that the minimum wage would cost jobs ... I have simply accepted that econometric models indicate a potential jobs impact.
Independent, *1991*

*

The goal of economic policy must be to raise the standard of living and provide a decent quality of life for all. This requires

active government, ready to intervene for the common interest and create a partnership for economic success.
Change and National Renewal *(Blair leadership manifesto), 23 June 1994*

*

Britain does not invest enough. Short-term relationships between companies and shareholders are partly to blame: dividends are high in the UK and sometimes do not reflect profitability.
Speech in Birmingham, 30 June 1994

*

Full employment need not be a mirage.
Change and National Renewal *(Blair leadership manifesto), June 1994*

*

The new establishment is not a meritocracy, but a power elite of money-shifters, middle men and speculators ... people whose self interest will always come before the national or the public interest. If they are allowed to go on running the country in their interests, is it any wonder that it is not run in ours?
Speech to the Labour Party Conference, 4 October 1994

*

I reject protectionism as wrong and impractical.
Speech in Tokyo, 5 January 1996

*

The mirror image of the economic insecurity is a profound sense of social, even moral insecurity ... social and family ties

have loosened. Communities which changed little from one generation to the next have collapsed.
Ibid.

*

Serious change was required to improve competitiveness at the end of the 1970s. The emphasis on enterprise, on initiative and incentive and on tackling lack of responsiveness in the public sector was necessary.
Speech in New York, 11 February 1996

*

I am passionately pro free trade and anti protectionist.
Speech in New York, 11 April 1996

*

We do not want to import the rigidities apparent in some European economies, particularly when Governments of left and right on the Continent are moving to change their systems to make them more flexible.
Speech in Birmingham, 3 July 1996

*

An over-rigid labour market in the end helps no one. Indeed, in some of its forms, it can be the enemy of social inclusion. What appears to be protecting some, may just be keeping others out.
Speech in Amsterdam, 24 January 1997

*

Progressive parties today are parties of fiscal responsibility and prudence. You do not do anything for anybody by making a wreckage of the economy.

29 May 1997

Taxation

[We will create] an immediate 50% increase in house-building. We'll retain tax relief on mortgages, making it easier for lower income groups to borrow and we'll cut house waiting-lists.
Tony Blair's Election Address, June 1983

*

Income tax cuts are the worst thing that can be done for the economy and the least effective way to provide jobs.
Hansard, *19 March 1987*

*

The second priority is to invest in health and education. We have said we will reverse the 2p tax cut. That will help pay for better services.
Northern Echo, *10 June 1987*

*

You have to decide where you're going to hit people in taxation terms, and if you hit too low, if you hit too many people, you're going to lose.
BBC TV, 17 January 1993

*

We're going to stop the Tory game of one-penny-up or one-penny-down, abstracting income tax from the rest of the economy.
BBC TV, 26 June 1994

*

A low-success economy is a high-tax one.
Speech in Birmingham, 30 June 1994

*

There are top-rate taxpayers now who are hardly in the super-rich bracket and I think we've got to be extremely sensitive to them.
New Statesman, *15 July 1994*

*

An incompetent economy ends you up with higher taxes.
Interview on Walden, *LWT, 24 July 1994*

*

If you ever want to know whose side the Tories are on, look at the tax system.
Speech to Labour Party Conference, 4 October 1994

*

Tax should be fair. It should be related to ability to pay.
Ibid.

*

We will take the profits of the new robber barons of Tory Britain in the privatized utilities and use them for the most radical programme of work and education ever put forward in Britain.
Speech to Labour Party Conference, 3 October 1995

*

We all want ordinary hard-working families to pay less tax. But the way to cut tax, is to cut unemployment, cut crime, cut welfare spending – all the reasons taxes have gone up.
Ibid.

*

Penal rates of taxation do not make economic or political sense. They are gone for good.
Speech to CBI Conference, 13 November 1995

*

I want a tax regime where through hard work, risk and success, people can become wealthy.
Speech to TUC Conference, 13 November 1995

*

If there are any tax rates that we have in mind we will be open and honest with people about them ... We aren't going into the election and tell lies like the Conservatives.
BBC TV, 14 November 1995

*

New Labour is not an old-style tax-and-spend party but wants a tax system that is fair, that rewards enterprise, at the

bottom as well as the top income levels.
Speech to Time Magazine *Dinner, 30 November 1995*

*

John Humphrys: Are you going to be able to achieve everything you're promising without any increases in taxation at
all? It beggars belief, doesn't it?
Tony Blair: No, it doesn't beggar belief.
BBC Radio, 22 December 1995

*

We have said, quite rightly, that we don't want high marginal
rates of tax at the top income levels, because it acts as a disin-
centive, the same is precisely true at the bottom of the income
scale.
Ibid.

*

The idea is that you take the excess profits that have been made
by the privatized utilities as a result of the way they've been
privatized, you take some of those excess profits, and it's well
established they're there, and you put them in a special dedicated fund in order to fund [Welfare-to-Work] programmes.
BBC TV, 12 January 1996

*

A high tax economy is not a high success economy.
Speech in Swansea, 10 May 1996

*

No party, sensitive to the changed times, is going to want to

raise taxes as a matter of principle.
Speech in Cape Town, 14 October 1996

*

Sometimes our political opponents portray the Labour Party
as a bunch of kill-joys, always opposing tax cuts and increases
in living standards. Nothing could be further from the truth
. . . we want people to pay lower taxes.
LIFFE Lecture, 16 October 1996

*

We will be open with the people about tax.
BBC Radio, 4 November 1996

*

Now if there are any changes on tax or spending that we want
to make we will disclose them well in advance of the general
election.
BBC Radio, 27 November 1996

*

There are no concealed tax increases . . . There is no evasion,
no double-dealing, no hidden agenda.
Leading Britain into the Future, Press Conference, 8 January 1997

*

I am not going into the election with anybody saying there is
any hidden agenda anywhere . . . There is not a single hidden
spending commitment anywhere. Any spending commitment

that we have is properly financed, that means there are no tax
increases implied by the programme.
BBC Radio, 8 January 1997

*

We will not raise the basic and top rates of income tax.
Labour's local government conference, 8 February 1997

*

A windfall levy today to cut the bills of social security tomor-
row.
Speech to Guardian/*Nexus Conference, 1 March 1997*

*

Labour want their taxes low just like everyone else.
Speech to Labour Gala Dinner, 12 March 1997

*

We have no spending promises which require tax increases
except the windfall levy on the excess profits of the privatized
utilities.
Sun, *25 March 1997*

*

Today marks the burial of tax-and-spend politics from Labour.
Labour Election Press Conference, 26 March 1997

Privatization

Ownership of shares is just having a stack of chips on the casino table.

The Times, *27 October 1987*

*

Public utilities like Telecom and Gas and essential industries such as British Airways and Rolls Royce were sold off by the Tories in the closest thing, post-war, to legalized political corruption. What we all owned was taken away from us, flogged off at a cheap price to win votes and the proceeds used to fund tax cuts. In fact it was a unique form of corruption, since we were bribed with our own money.

Describing the privatization of public utilities, News on Sunday, *1 November 1987*

*

The privatization of electricity is running into serious difficulties. The bill will mean rising prices, a nuclear tax and now the public will even have to bear the cost of nuclear waste disposal.

Guardian, *25 November 1988*

*

*

We will speak up for a country that knows the good sense of
a public industry in public hands.
Hansard, *speech on Electricity Bill, 12 December 1988*

*

We are proud that we took the industry into public ownership. When we come to power, it will be reinstated as a public
service for the people of this country, and will not be run for
private profit.
On the privatization of British Airways, Hansard, *12 December 1988*

*

A scandalous and undemocratic measure.
Ibid.

*

The Government have failed miserably to persuade the
majority of people in this country that the proposal [to priva-
tize the electricity industry] is good. At the next election, they
shall pay the price for that misjudgement.
Hansard, *10 April 1989*

*

The great utilities must be treated as public services and
should be owned by the public.
July 1989

*

In place of that tired Tory agenda for the Eighties – privatization, pollution, price rises – we give the country a new vision for the Nineties where conserving energy is as important as producing it.

Speech from the floor to Labour Conference, October 1989

*

If you can't achieve something through ownership, you achieve it through proper regulation and control because these are often monopoly services that people depend on.

BBC TV, 12 June 1994

*

I think the British people think that to have sold off the water industry is absolutely wrong.

Ibid.

*

What we need is the most efficient public service possible for the customers. I was against these industries being privatized but I do not believe that, with all the problems in our health and education and police services, the most pressing priority for an incoming Labour government would be to spend large sums of money to buy up shares in the privatized utilities.

Sunday Mirror, 26 June 1994

*

We've got to end this insane notion that everything's got to be shoved into the private sector. There are decent public services. And they should be kept as public services.

ITV, 100 Women, 10 July 1994

*

I am not going to get into a situation where I am declaring that the Labour government is going to commit sums of money to re-nationalization several years down the line.
January 1995

*

We will fight to keep our railways as a proper public service, publicly owned and accountable to the people.
Speech at Methodist Central Hall, 29 April 1995

*

We will give Britain a modern integrated transport network, built in partnership between public and private finance and restoring a unified system of railways with a publicly owned, publicly accountable BR at its core.
Speech to Labour Party Conference, 1 October 1996

*

I certainly believe that where there is no overriding reason for preferring the public provision of goods and services, particularly where those services operate in a commercial market, then the presumption should be that economic activity is best left to the private sector, with market forces being fully encouraged to operate.
Speech at the Corn Exchange, 7 April 1997

The Environment

Labour's environmental vision is of a high wage, high skill economy with high environmental standards.
Speech to the Royal Society, 27 February 1996

*

Labour has, of course, always believed that good government means good environmental government.
Ibid.

*

High environmental standards could improve rather than damage our competitiveness.
Ibid.

*

I love our countryside.
Country Life, *26 September 1996*

*

Bringing up children in the country is a million times better

than in towns. For small and obvious reasons: the facilities are far better.
Ibid.

*

The great evil – although for country people, a necessary one – is road traffic. I don't know how you can control it.
Ibid.

*

As we say in the new Clause 4: 'We will work for a healthy environment which we protect, enhance and hold in trust for future generations.'
Speech to Labour Party Conference, 3 October 1996

*

I am not interested in demonizing the car.
Speech to a Transport conference, 4 February 1997

Part Three

A HAND UP – NOT A HAND-OUT

Tough on Crime

No one but a fool would excuse the rioting that disfigured our inner cities . . . but no one but a Tory would ignore the social despair in which such evil breeds.

Speech to the Labour Party Conference, October 1991

*

When young men and women seek but do not find any reflection of their hopes in the society around them, when the Tories create a creed of acquisition and place it alongside a culture without opportunity, when communities disintegrate and people within them feel they have no chance to improve and nothing to strive for, then it takes not a degree in social science, merely a modicum of common sense, to see that in the soil of alienation, crime will take root.

Speech to the Labour Party Conference, October 1992

*

Labour really is the genuine Party of law and order in Britain today.

Speech to Daily Mirror/Tribune *Conference, 19 January 1993*

*

It's a bargain – we give opportunity, we demand responsibility. There is no excuse for crime. None.
Article in the Sun, *3 March 1993*

*

Labour is the party of law and order in Britain today. Tough on crime and tough on the causes of crime.
Speech to the Labour Party Conference, 30 September 1993

*

No one but a fool would excuse crime on the basis of social conditions.
Ibid.

*

I believe victims must be consulted on any decision by the Crown Prosecution Service to drop or reduce the seriousness of a charge.
Sun, *17 December 1993*

*

Effective criminal justice must be backed up with effective measures of prevention. Let us be clear. Prison will be necessary for those that are a danger to the public. But a policy of 'prison works' as if putting people in gaol was the answer to rising crime, is an absurdity.
Press Release, 19 January 1994

*

Of course the victim should be put centre stage. Then let them drop the proposals to abolish the Criminal Injuries Compensation Scheme which will mean thousands of victims losing any right to decent compensation for crime.
Speech in Glasgow, 5 February 1994

*

Being tough on crime and tough on the causes of crime is not an empty slogan.
Change and National Renewal, 23 *June 1994*

*

We need to tackle crime's underlying causes like ... high levels of unemployment.
Sunday Mirror, 26 *June 1994*

*

Take the decriminalization of soft drugs. I haven't attempted to suppress that debate, but I don't believe the case is made out. I think the danger is that if you decriminalize cannabis, as has happened in Holland, you just become the focus for very hard drugs from all over the rest of Europe.
New Statesman *and* Society, 15 *July 1994*

*

We've opposed completely the abolition of the right to silence. We opposed the Government's laws on trespass. We

opposed the manner in which they are going to deal with
juvenile offenders.
Ibid.

*

I do believe that there would be less crime under Labour – I
believe that absolutely sincerely.
BBC TV, 3 October 1994

*

The unemployed youngster has no right to steal your radio.
But let's get just as serious about catching the people in the
City with an eye on your pension.
Speech to Labour Party Conference, 4 October 1994

*

We need to continue to crack down on the use of knives and
firearms . . . we need to ensure proper punishment for crimes
like rape and racial violence that are not properly dealt with.
Most important of all, however, we need to increase the likelihood that someone committing a crime will be caught.
Faith in the City – Ten Years On Speech, 29 January 1996

*

The real problem is not the hard-pressed single mum or
pensioner putting a 'treat' in their pocket rather than their
shopping-basket, the problem is organized gangs who choose
to make a living from this sort of crime.
Speech to the British Retail Consortium, 14 February 1996

*

There must be a comprehensive attack on crime and its causes instead of a search for easy headlines.
The Times, *4 November 1996*

*

We won't [scrap Tory immigration laws]. Under this Government, thousands of people every year settled in Britain illegally. We are determined to clamp down on this.
Sun, *25 March 1997*

Health and Welfare

We'll link pensions to average earnings.
Tony Blair's Election Address, June 1983

*

The real criticism of what the Prime Minister [John Major] has done [in attacking beggars] is not only its vindictiveness against someone who will be genuinely destitute, it is the notion that this is what we should be concentrating on. It is the pettiness and small-mindedness of it which will affront people and bewilder them when there are such massive problems to tackle, and when the Prime Minister appears to be oblivious to them.
Guardian, *30 May 1994*

*

I want to protect state pensions.
Daily Mirror, *26 June 1994*

*

A large social security budget is not a sign of Socialist success

but a necessary consequence of economic failure.
Speech in Southampton, 13 July 1994

*

Instead of cutting benefit, why not cut the homeless queue, cut unemployment, and build the houses?
Speech to Labour Party Conference, 4 October 1994

*

A nation at work, not on benefit. That is our pledge.
Speech to Labour Party Conference, 4 October 1994

*

Social aims without economic means are empty wishes. By uniting the two we can build a better future for all our people.
Mais Lecture, 22 May 1995

*

If we want to make flexible working a reality, then we must have a flexible welfare state. If we want single parents to achieve financial independence, then we must help them find training and childcare.
Speech to Opportunity 2000, 31 October 1995

*

In today's Britain no one should have to sleep rough on the streets.
Evening Standard, *20 December 1995*

*

New Labour's agenda for health ... is an agenda based on sensible change, not ideological dogma. It is about working with doctors, nurses and managers, not imposing change upon them.
Daily Express, *20 June 1996*

*

What does the average unemployed person need? ... They need a job, they don't need a few extra pounds on benefit.
BBC TV, 1 September 1996

*

He [Gordon Brown] has also said child benefit should not be paid to over-sixteens unless they genuinely attend schools. He is right.
Speech in Cape Town, 14 October 1996

*

Obviously some people will interpret this in a way which is harsh and unpleasant but I think the basic principle here is to say: yes it is right to be intolerant of people homeless on the streets.
Big Issue, *January 1997*

*

And as the bills of unemployment, family breakdown and low pay pile up, all the New Right can think of doing is to cut benefits to hold costs down.
Speech in Amsterdam, 24 January 1997

*

Education and welfare are the key tasks of an incoming Labour Government. They are the route both to increased prosperity and social justice, in the modern world.
Ibid.

*

There will be no option of a life permanently on full benefit. Where there is a suitable offer, people will be expected to take this up.
Ibid.

*

I know of children in my own constituency whose fathers don't work and whose grandfathers haven't worked. Once that starts, drug abuse starts happening, you get family instability and a whole range of problems.
Big Issue, *January 1997*

*

So I can say today for the long-term unemployed turning down all choices and staying on benefit – doing nothing, will not be an option.
Speech to Guardian/Nexus *Conference, 1 March 1997*

*

The next election is a choice about the National Health Service. Saving it with Labour. Destroying it under the Conservatives.
Speech to the Scottish Labour Party Conference, 7 March 1997

Education, Education, Education

[The Conservative Party] propose allowing schools to 'opt-out' of the local education system . . . The parents who lose the vote will have to lump it or try to find schooling elsewhere . . . Schools once out of the system will be free to choose where the pupils come from.
Northern Echo, *10 June 1987*

*

The net result of the measures outlined in the Queen's Speech will be to favour those who are already doing well and to deepen social division. Schools in well-to-do areas will leave local authority control. They will raise, through voluntary contributions, additional resources to buy better teachers and better facilities. They will introduce entrance exams and tests. The end will resemble a subsidized private school.
Letter to The Times, *1 July 1987*

*

It's parents who bring up kids, not governments.
Article in the Sun, *3 March 1993*

*

It's absolutely vital that parents get as much information as possible. I certainly want that for my children; I want to know exactly how they're performing at school; I want to have a proper assessment of them. But the difference between ourselves and the government has been not over the principles of these issues but the way that they're implemented.
BBC TV, 26 June 1994

*

I have no problem at all with comparing schools, I think that is entirely sensible and natural.
Ibid..

*

I wonder if it isn't time to recognize that three A-Levels are too narrow for the third of pupils who do them, and the A-Level system, which condemns two-thirds of pupils to vocational courses deemed second-class, is at odds with the demands of a modern economy and modern society.
Speech in Manchester, 4 July 1994

*

In our project of national renewal, education renewal must be at the forefront. Our watchwords will be aspiration, opportunity and achievement.
Ibid.

*

There is no more honourable a profession than that of a teacher.
Ibid.

*

Under the new system schools choose children instead of parents choosing schools.
Ibid.

*

We need to balance the desire of parents, teachers and governors to have power of decision-making within their schools, with the interests of local communities in preserving the standards of those schools for the parents and children of future generations to come.
Ibid.

*

The employment deficit, the equality deficit, the opportunity deficit, the security deficit – none will be overcome until we eliminate the education deficit.
Ibid.

*

For every school, fair and equal funding. No return to selection, academic or social.
Speech to Labour Party Conference, 3 October 1995

*

Teachers should be properly rewarded. But if they can't do their job, they should not be teaching at all.
Ibid.

*

New guidelines on homework – thirty minutes minimum
from age seven, ninety minutes from eleven – will require
parents to ensure it is done ... There must be pressure, too,
on parents. Their responsibilities will be spelt out in
home–school contracts.
Daily Mail, *5 December 1995*

*

There will be no change to the Labour Party policy on selection, no going back to dividing our children into successes
and failures, no going back from our commitment to comprehensive education.
Daily Mirror, *25 January 1996*

*

I never try and tell people what to do for their own children.
BBC Radio, 29 January 1996

*

Education will be the passion of my government.
Speech at National Film Theatre, 2 May 1996

*

Ask me my main three priorities for government and I will
tell you: education, education and education.
Speech to Labour Party Conference, 3 October 1996

*

There should be zero tolerance of failure in Britain's schools.
Ibid.

*

Education should be a leading office of state, comparable to the other departments which have traditionally had that title.
Speech at Ruskin College, 16 December 1996

*

School failure is an educational catastrophe. We need to be able to intervene early with sufficient power to stop the spiral decline. One new way forward would be for good well-led effectively run schools to take over schools that LEAs identify as heading for failure.
Ibid.

*

The average length of time in office for ministers of education since the First World War is less than two years ... It has got to change. Under Labour, it will. I want my ministers to expect to take responsibility for seeing a strategy through and to take the credit, too, if they succeed.
Ibid.

*

The Tories' neglect of the country's stock of school buildings has been serious ... I am delighted that David Blunkett was, after exhaustive discussions with the banks, able to announce at Easter a new public–private partnership to refurbish and improve groups of schools ... we will make a start. And we will follow through.
Ibid.

*

In primary schools we should have proper base-line assessment, assessing each pupil as they come into school to see what they need.
BBC TV, 12 January 1997

*

Education will be the first priority of the Labour government. It will be the first Bill of the first Queen's Speech.
Ibid.

*

We want every school in the country to have what's called a home–school contract between the school and the parents so that parents and pupils and teachers know exactly what is demanded in relation to each child and as part of that we want to make sure that there are proper national guidelines for homework.
Ibid.

*

To say that because education will be our number one priority in government, we are downgrading the other parts of our programme ... is frankly absurd.
Guardian, 15 January 1997

*

We intend to extend choice.
Sun, 25 March 1997

Don't Do as I Do ...

Many people in politics believe that the reason Tony Blair is obsessed by education is his own experience as a parent. The controversy over the Blairs' choice of school for their son Euan, and the ensuing row over Harriet Harman's decision to bus her child across London to school have left deep scars. Many in the Labour movement will never forgive either of them for putting their children ahead of their politics. Sick, but true. The Harman crisis was probably Blair's biggest challenge during his period as Leader of the Opposition. He knew if he gave in to demands from within his own Party and from his opponents for her head, he would be left dangerously exposed. He knows now that having given education policy such prominence, his government may well be judged on whether our schools are better at educating our children at the end of his term of office or not.

*

Parents are going to choose whatever is the best choice of school for their kids. We have disagreed with the government opting out schools, but you can't say to parents they then can't choose them – that would be manifestly absurd.

BBC TV, 26 June 1994

*

Any parent wants the best for their children. I am not going to make a choice for my child on the basis of what is the politically correct thing to do.
BBC TV, 1 December 1994

*

Well I think everyone wants to do the best for their children.
Desert Island Discs, *23 November 1996*

On the Harman Affair

This issue, however, is no longer about Harriet and her child but how we handle ourselves in this difficult period. Let me make it clear what it is about. The Tories are trying to turn the education of an eleven-year-old boy into a party political football. They want a scalp as their prize. If they get it don't think they will stop there. They will go on to the next and the next.
Speech to Parliamentary Labour Party, 25 January 1996

*

The time has come to pull together, to get behind the whole of the shadow cabinet and to stand firm because the Tories are not going to succeed in making this a political football.
Daily Telegraph, *25 January 1996*

*

I feel very strongly about this. If the degree of furore is going to determine whether someone stays or goes, that is a very dangerous principle. It is a principle this government is led by.

Daily Mirror, *26 January 1996*

*

A politician who does not try within their principles to do the best for their child is a politician who is in danger of losing touch with humanity.

Ibid.

*

I have had enough of yielding to these bastards. They are not going to have a scalp.

Reacting to Tory calls for Harriet Harman's dismissal over her choice of school for her son

Part Four

IT'S A WONDERFUL WORLD

Europe

Blair the Europhobe

Above all, the EEC takes away Britain's freedom to follow the sort of economic policies we need. These are just two reasons for coming out. Only a Labour government will do it.
Tony Blair By-Election Leaflet, 1982

*

Labour is not anti-European. But the EEC has pushed up prices, especially food ... Above all, the EEC takes away Britain's freedom to follow the sort of economic policies we need. These are just two of the reasons for coming out. Only a Labour government will do it.
Beaconsfield By-election Address, 1982

*

We'll negotiate a withdrawal from the EEC which has drained our natural resources and destroyed jobs.
Sedgefield Election Address, 1983

*

Each piece of legislation will be judged on its merits. I have no intention whatever of agreeing to anything and everything that emerges from the EU.
Speech to the CBI Annual Conference, 13 November 1995

*

Contrary to the myths peddled by the Tory Lie Machine, Labour does not believe in signing up to everything that comes out of Brussels.
Sun, *1 May 1996*

*

I shall defend the interests of the British people as stubbornly and fiercely as I expect the German government to defend the German interests.
Speech in Bonn, 18 July 1996

*

I have made it absolutely clear and let me repeat to you again that if it is in Britain's interests to be isolated through the use of the national veto then we will be isolated.
BBC Radio, 15 December 1996

*

We will lead in Europe, rather than get pushed around.
Sun, *5 February 1997*

*

We would not join in any fudged single currency or one not
in Britain's interest – period.
2 April 1997

*

Of course there are emotional issues involved in the single
currency. It's not just a question of economics. It's about the
sovereignty of Britain and constitutional issues too.
Sun, *17 April 1997*

Blair the Europhile

The Government's refusal to countenance the basic social
rights in the [Social] Charter severely undermines the interests
of British employees, and the irrational conduct and bad faith
that characterizes our isolation in Europe profoundly damage
Britain's interests abroad. By their opposition to the Social
Charter, far from assisting job creation, the Government will
harm the long-term prospects for British employment.
Hansard, *Social Charter Debate, 29 November 1989*

*

We can prepare ourselves for a new role as part of the mainstream in Europe.
Speech to the Labour Party Conference, September 1990

*

The best of Europe for Britain. And the best of Britain for
Europe.
Ibid.

*

A Labour Government would lift the British veto on the Social Charter and support the extension of qualified majority voting on social affairs. We could then consider sensibly the manner of implementing these principles.
Press Release, 2 December 1991

*

What you're doing is pointing out what the policy of the Party was in the 1983 election and the reason that many of us, like myself, fought to change that policy was precisely because we recognized that it was not in the interests of the country.
BBC Radio, 29 May 1994

*

I don't deny that there are those in the Labour Party who still hold to the position of 1983.
Ibid.

*

I have always believed that our country can prosper best within Europe. Along with Neil Kinnock and John Smith I believed that Labour should be committed to close co-operation with Europe so that we all may benefit. And I helped change party policy in this area.
Sunday Mirror, *26 June 1994*

*

Britain's interests demand that this country is at the forefront

of the development of the new Europe.
Speech to Labour Party Conference, 4 October 1994

*

Under my leadership I will never allow this country to be isolated or left behind in Europe.
Ibid.

*

I always believed it was important for Britain to be in Europe.
December 1994

*

We should consider extending Qualified Majority Voting in certain areas such as social, environmental, industrial and regional policy.
Speech to Royal Institute of International Affairs, 5 April 1995

*

We are prepared to consider extending Qualified Majority Voting, where it is in our interests to do so, in areas of social, environmental, industrial and regional policy, especially if there is a re-weighting of QMV.
Speech in Bonn, 30 May 1995

*

It is true that the policies of the Labour Party were withdrawal from the European Community, when I first stood for Parliament in 1983. Now, as a matter of fact, I had already

indicated to my constituency party that I opposed that policy and would fight to reverse it.
BBC Radio, 7 June 1995

*

The Right argue that further integration in Europe would lead to the loss of Britain's separate identity, sovereignty and freedom of action. The argument is based on delusion.
Speech to NewsCorp, 17 July 1995

*

To be sidelined without influence is not a betrayal of Europe. It is a betrayal of Britain.
Speech to Labour Party Conference, 3 October 1995

*

We are in Europe not because it is in Europe's interest but because it is Britain's interest.
Sun, 1 May 1996

*

Our policy will be pro-European.
Ibid.

*

I think it is important that we keep the option, all the options open.
On a Single Currency, BBC Radio, 13 December 1996

*

The Labour Party is clear that we do not want to leave the EU
. . . No serious part of the Labour Party wants to withdraw.
What the Papers Say, *21 February 1997*

*

This is Tony Blair Day in Europe.
Italian journalist to Tony Blair at EU Summit press conference, 23 May 1997

*

A Britain that is leading in Europe is a Britain capable of ever-
closer relations also with the United States of America.
During summit with President Clinton, 29 May 1997

The World

Asian countries will be more interested in increasing ties with Britain if we have influence in Europe. A Britain without influence in Europe is a Britain less valuable as a partner.
Speech to NewsCorp, 17 July 1995

*

The economic success of the Tigers came not as a result of low state spending, low taxes or even open markets. The real reasons are investment, savings and skills. In Korea, gross savings account for 37% of GDP, in Taiwan 28% of GDP, in Japan 33%. In Britain it is 12.8%.
Sunday Times, *29 October 1995*

*

The argument, because the Asian Tigers spend a lower proportion of GDP they enjoy greater economic success than the UK is simplistic, but wrong.
Ibid.

*

The Commonwealth is too great an asset to let slide away in

the way that successive Tory governments have done.
Evening Standard, *8 November 1995*

*

It is not necessary to turn our back on Europe to be pro-Commonwealth. In fact the two should reinforce each other. If we are leaders in Europe our influence in the Commonwealth will be greater. If we play our leadership role in the commonwealth to the full we will maximize our influence in Europe.
Ibid.

*

Let me say this clearly: America is crucial to European security and it always will be. The UK and the US will always turn to each other in times of crisis. The UK will always be the country the US turns to when it needs military support, as in the Gulf. The special relationship between Britain and the US will always be one of special trust. And it must play a crucial role in binding together Europe and America.
Speech to Time Magazine *Dinner, 30 November 1995*

*

We are patriotic, but we will always stand up against aggression against someone else.
29 January 1996

*

I have always been a strong believer in the Commonwealth, often an unfashionable thing to be ... I am determined not to let a priceless legacy like this fade into nostalgia.
On the Commonwealth, Speech in Cape Town, 14 October 1996

*

Ours is the first generation able to contemplate the possibility that we may live our entire lives without going to war or sending our children to war. That is a prize beyond value.
Speaking at the NATO Summit, 27 May 1997

Defence

I want a negotiated settlement and I believe that given the starkness of the military options we need to compromise on certain things. I don't think that ultimately the wishes of the Falkland Islanders must determine our position.
Sunday Telegraph, *9 May 1982*

*

We don't need dangerous and costly Trident and Cruise missiles, which just escalate the nuclear arms race.
Tony Blair's 1983 General Election Address

*

Parliamentary Labour CND supports the removal of all nuclear weapons from British territory and expresses solidarity with all campaigners for peace.
Sanity Advert signed by Tony Blair, May 1986

*

It is the primary responsibility of any government to defend the country. That much is obvious. But my contention here is

that a strong defence capability is an essential part of Britain's foreign policy.
Daily Telegraph, *3 February 1997*

*

I am saying quite clearly to you that it is not the case that the military or indeed any other group of people can simply exercise a veto on those that come into their profession and those that do not ... I have said that the principle is that people should not be discharged from the military simply on the basis that they're gay.
BBC Radio, *10 May 1996*

*

New Labour is not a unilateralist party.
Sun, *25 March 1997*

Part Five

OLD LABOUR, NEW LABOUR

The Labour Party

I'm basically a centrist in the party, and want to see it united.
South Bucks Observer, *8 April 1982*

*

Just so there is no further misunderstanding: I support the Labour Party's present leadership; Labour's plan for jobs; withdrawal from the EEC (certainly unless the most fundamental changes are effected); and nuclear disarmament, unilaterally if necessary; in particular I intend to campaign against Trident and American-controlled cruise missiles on our soil. I do so as a Labour Party man, not as a Bennite or any other 'ite'.
Letter to the South Bucks Observer, *who had accused him of being a 'Benn-backer', 16 April 1982*

*

One can tell it [Sedgefield] is different because it is the place where the SDP ceases telling people that it represents the Labour Party of Attlee and Gaitskell and begins saying that it represents the Tory Party of Butler and Macmillan.
Maiden Speech in the House of Commons, 6 July 1983

*

The local party grows out of – and is part of – local life. That is its strength. That is why my constituents are singularly unimpressed when told that the Labour Party is extreme. They see extremism more as an import from outside that is destroying their livelihoods.
Ibid.

*

The political wing of Sainsbury's.
Blair's description of the SDP

*

I thought I told him not to say that.
Upon being told that Labour MP Dennis Canavan had called him authoritarian

*

Interviewer: What makes an Old Fettesian become a Labour MP?
Tony Blair: A catalogue of errors and mistakes.
Fettes School Magazine, *December 1991*

*

My press releases read like essays until Gordon [Brown] showed me how to write them.
Sunday Times, *17 July 1992*

*

To change our country, we must show that we have the courage to change ourselves.
Guardian, *9 June 1993*

*

I don't think the character of any party becomes clear until
you're in power.
The Spectator, 1 October 1994

*

Parties that do not change die, and this party is a living
movement, not an historical monument.
Speech to Labour Party Conference, 4 October 1994

*

Our Party. New Labour. Our mission. New Britain. New
Labour New Britain. New Britain!
Closing words to his Party Conference Speech, 4 October 1994

*

Those who seriously believe we cannot improve on words
written for the world of 1918 when we are now in 1995 are not
learning from our history but living it.
On Clause 4, 11 January 1995

*

With my class background, if all I had wanted to do was to
exercise power I could and would – let's be blunt about this –
have joined another party.
Interview in Vanity Fair, March 1995

*

What modernization to me is about is not dumping principle.

It's the opposite. It's retrieving what the Labour Party is really about.
19 April 1995

*

I know my Labour Party very well now. It may be a strange thing to say but before I became leader I did not.
Guardian, *July 1995*

*

In other European countries the Labour Party would be called the Social Democratic Party. The values are the same.
Evening Standard, *21 September 1995*

*

What you have to remember is that those who are running the save Clause Four campaign – the Campaign Group and the NUM – those are the people who were in charge of the Labour Party in the early 1980s, when it nearly went out of existence.
Interview in the Observer, *1995*

*

I place before you my vision of a new Britain. A nation reborn. Prosperous, secure, united. One Britain. New Labour. New Britain.
Start of Speech to Labour Party Conference, 3 October 1995

*

New Labour. New Britain. The party renewed. The country reborn. New Labour. New Britain.
Conclusion of Speech to Labour Party Conference, 3 October 1995

*

I love my party. I just hate it being in opposition.
Speech to Labour Party Conference, 3 October 1995

*

I know that for some of you, New Labour has been painful. There is no greater pain to be endured in politics than the birth of a new idea.
Ibid.

*

My project will be complete when the Labour Party learns to love Peter Mandelson.
Attributed quote in the Daily Telegraph, *2 March 1996*

*

I want everyone in the country to realize that the programme of the Labour Party is agreed by every constituent part of the Labour Party. That is, if you like, our contract with the British people.
BBC TV, 31 March 1996

*

I'm not going to trade with any group or faction.
Ibid.

*

I think you should always put the national interest before any

section of interest in your own party.
Ibid.

*

I never try and spin people a line on this, there is an element
within the Labour Party, though much smaller than people
think, that disagrees with the modernization drive of the
Labour Party.
Ibid.

*

The actual legislative programme that I announced last week
is not actually to cut out the party conference or anyone else,
it will be a programme that actually involves all the
constituent elements of the Labour Party.
Ibid.

*

The solutions of neither the old Left nor the new Right will
do. We need a radical centre in modern politics and today's
Labour Party – New Labour – is a party of the centre as well
as the centre-left.
Speech to the British-American Chamber of Commerce, 11 April 1996

*

It is New Labour that is the One Nation party today. New
Labour, a party of One Nation Radicals.
Speech in Swansea, 10 May 1996

*

There is no one in the world more powerful today than a

member of a focus group.
Sunday Telegraph, *24 June 1996*

*

If you look at Labour's policies, no one can conceivably say that's a cautious programme. It's a very radical programme.
Interview in the New Statesman, *5 July 1996*

*

Most people aren't daft. They understood that the party had to change.
Ibid.

*

If every time you're subjected to a bit of criticism and then you simply cave in under it, well, what a hopeless form of leadership that is.
BBC TV, 1 September 1996

*

The way we make policy is now more open, more rational, more considered.
Speech in Cape Town, 14 October 1996

*

I would miss my family and whatnot, and I hope that my Party would miss me. You know, the National Executive would pass a resolution by twenty votes to five asking me to return.
On what he would miss on his desert island, Desert Island Discs, *23 November 1996*

*

What we have done is to take the basic values of the Labour Party but apply them to a world that is completely changed.
BBC TV, 19 December 1996

*

As the party membership grows, as we've many party people now that are involved in business, small business, from all different walks of life, we can have a far more mature, sensible discussion.'
BBC TV, 29 January 1997

*

We will consult our membership much more, but the membership itself will be representative of the ordinary people of this country.
Ibid.

*

Our decision-making structures set to be revitalized to place more power in the hands of ordinary members. Our democracy revived by One Member One Vote.
Speech to Labour Local Government Conference, 8 February 1997

*

All MPs are selected by ordinary Party members, not small committees.
Speech to the Newspaper Society, 10 March 1997

*

Do not underestimate the significance of a doubled member-
ship. It puts us in touch with real people, real communities.
This is a party of the people, not of pressure groups.
Speech to London Gala Dinner, 12 March 1997

*

It's not a sin to try to get elected, though I know people regard
this as not the constitutional function of the Labour Party.
15 April 1997

Why Labour Lost and Lost and Lost and Lost

In fact, most people share Labour's values and dislike those of the Conservatives. Rather, the problem has been a perception that Labour's policies and attitudes did not faithfully reflect its own values, combined with doubts about its competence.
The Times, *29 September 1987*

*

A vacuum is opening up into which Labour, as the party of intervention, can move. But it must recognize two things: it cannot design its policies to appeal simply to its own producer interests – in any event, trade unionists are consumers and citizens too; and it must use government intervention as an instrument to promote choice, not uniformity.
The Times, *5 January 1988*

*

We were very aware when we first came into Parliament that the Labour Party was in tremendous trouble with certain attitudes that made it unelectable, and those things had to change. And of course there was an electoral advantage in doing so. But it's quite wrong to say as a result of desiring to change those things that you are merely people governed by electoral instinct rather than any system of fundamental beliefs.

Guardian, *29 June 1991*

*

The policy review was a necessary exercise. But, perhaps unavoidably, it tended to establish more clearly what Labour no longer stood for – what it was not – rather than what it is.

Guardian, *30 June 1992*

*

Winning the next election for Labour requires not a delicate shift in tactics or strategy, but a project. It should start with the Labour Party's historic principles, the values that define its identity. It should then apply them, for the modern world, to both its policies and its organization.

Ibid.

*

After the '79 election the Labour Party dived off in the wrong direction and thought, well the reason we haven't succeeded is that we haven't offered really fundamental socialism to the people in the way we wrote it thirty or forty years ago. Well, of course, that was the opposite of the truth. The truth was that the people were actually questioning the pale imitation of it, never mind wanting the full red-blooded core of it.

Sunday Times, *19 July 1992*

*

The worry of the electorate in 1992 was not that Labour had changed, but the concern was that the change was superficial ... The reason Labour lost in 1992, as for the previous three elections, is not complex, it is simple: society had changed and we did not change sufficiently with it ... Labour does need a clear identity based on principle, not a series of adjustments with each successive electoral defeat.
Renewal, *October 1992*

*

Since the [1992] election, I have said all the way through that the Labour Party has to ask itself this question: 'Did we lose because we did change or did we lose because we didn't change enough?' In my view, we lost because we were not sufficiently perceived to be in tune with the aspirations, the ambitions of people.
Scotsman, *12 February 1993*

*

The Labour Party got into problems [in the early 1980s] when, like many left-of-centre parties, it ... started to confuse ... principles and values with particular means of implementation, which might be relevant for a particular time but which then have to change from generation to generation.
Financial Times, *11 June 1994*

*

The reason we have been out of power for fifteen years is simple – that society changed and we refused to change with it.
New Statesman, *15 July 1994*

*

I think one of the tragedies of the Left was that it allowed the term 'equality' to really become a term of abuse about levelling down.
BBC Radio, 14 December 1995

*

We have frankly admitted that we took far too long in the 1980s as a political party to face up to the need for change.
Tokyo, 5 January 1996

*

I remember going through the last two general elections, and there were all sorts of policies we had that the leadership collectively didn't want. I remember, during the last general election campaign, the pledges we had on child benefit. We all knew that by then the economic circumstances had changed and these were pledges that it really wasn't sensible to hold to.
Independent, *13 July 1996*

New Labour

Let us say what we mean and mean what we say. Not just what we are against. But what we are for. No more ditching. No more dumping. Stop saying what we don't mean. And start saying what we do mean. What we stand by, what we stand for.

Speech to Labour Party Conference, 4 October 1994

*

There are three clear tasks in the creation of New Labour. One is the clear reconstruction of a modern ideology. The second is to produce an organization that is fighting fit with a political culture that is open and welcoming . . . The third is to take the new aims and values and describe them, in terms of the ideas underpinning them and in the development of policy.

The Spectator, *22 March 1995*

*

Today a New Labour Party is being born. Our task now is nothing less than the rebirth of our nation. A new Britain.

National renewal ... New Labour being born. The task of
building new Britain now to come.
April 1995

*

My leadership is based on this central belief: that to become a
serious party of government again, the Labour Party required
not a series of adjustments but a quantum leap.
Speech to NewsCorp, 17 July 1995

*

By contrast the agenda of New Labour means a fundamental
change of attitude.
Speech to TUC Conference, 12 September 1995

*

In other European countries, the Labour Party would be
called the Social Democratic Party – the values are the same.
Evening Standard, 21 September 1995

*

1983 was, for me a watershed, New Labour was reborn then.
Speech to Labour Party Conference, 3 October 1995

*

The absolutely essential condition for a successful Labour
government is that we have a clear sense of what we want to
achieve and how we can achieve it ... the important thing is
that the programme and policy reflect the vision.
BBC Radio, 14 December 1995

*

I want the Labour Party to be seen as the party of business.
Speech in Tokyo, 5 January 1996

*

New Labour is not some public relations gimmick ... It is changed in opposition and it will remain changed in government.
BBC TV, 14 January 1996

*

New Labour does not believe it is the job of government to interfere in the running of business.
Speech to Nottingham Chamber of Commerce, 19 January 1996

*

The Labour Party has changed. It is almost literally a new party.
Speech to British Retail Consortium, 14 February 1996

*

It is Labour that offers the new British dream now. Labour that can build a new Britain that is fair, efficient and can regain our standing in the world. Labour that speaks for the majority.
Speech in Swansea, 10 May 1996

*

Today's Labour Party, New Labour, is the political embodiment of the changed world – the new challenges, the new

policies and the new politics – that I have described.
Speech in Bonn, 18 June 1996

*

The values of the Labour Party haven't changed . . . the values of the Labour Party are being applied afresh to the modern world . . . I'm absolutely convinced it is the right thing for the country.
BBC TV, 1 September 1996

*

In fact what we have done is to take the basic values of the Labour Party but apply them to a world that is completely changed.
BBC TV, 19 December 1996

*

To be able to reach out and build new support – that is the purpose of New Labour. Because if you don't do, what you become yourself, as a political party, is a glorified pressure group – which is what the Labour Party was for much of the eighties.
Big Issue, *January 1997*

Road to Victory

There was one thing that I really wanted to do, and I have been given the chance by you to do it. I only hope your faith in me will be repaid.

Letter to Party members following the 1983 General Election

*

Neil Kinnock:	I'd like you to go on the front bench.
Long silence.	
Neil Kinnock:	Don't you want to go to the front bench?
Tony Blair:	Yes. Yes, I do.
Neil Kinnock:	Well, listen, I want you to be in our team and that's that.
Tony Blair:	I want to be in the team, too.
Neil Kinnock:	What's the matter then?
Tony Blair:	I'm a bit surprised.

Neil Kinnock explaining Blair's reaction to his offer of promotion in November 1984 (quoted in Tony Blair *by John Rentoul)*

*

I'm still young. I've had some good breaks. I've been very lucky, but I'm acutely conscious of the fact that the history of

politics is littered with the P45s of those who were supposed to be rising stars and ended up being shooting stars.
Reacting to his election to the Shadow Cabinet, BBC TV, 21 November 1988

*

Our obvious sense of disappointment must be balanced by a sense of achievement, that we took so many seats in different parts of the country. But it was too much to do – so it now appears – to come from where we were in 1987 to actually win a majority.
Speaking the night after the 1992 Election, BBC TV, 10 April 1992

*

It's got to be Tony hasn't it?
John Smith to an aide, speculating on his successor three days before his death, 9 May 1994

*

But Gordon has wanted it so much. Much more than I ever have.
On the party leadership, May 1994

*

It was difficult discussing it obviously, and I had always assumed that he would be the Leader of the Labour Party, and I have always had a huge and still have a huge admiration for him . . . Once John died and we had to come to the decision, then we did discuss it and I think it is a market-measure of Gordon and the type of person he is, that in the end we were able to agree to it.
On his talks with Gordon Brown about running for the Party leadership, Desert Island Discs, *23 November 1996*

*

I can't think of any major policy differences between the three
of us.
On himself and leadership rivals Margaret Beckett and John Prescott, BBC
TV, 12 June 1994

*

What we're about is not remaining a party of opposition but
moving to be a party of government.
BBC TV, 12 June 1994

*

By re-establishing its core identity, the Labour Party and the
left can regain the intellectual self-confidence to take on and
win the battle of ideas. For too long, the left has thought it has
had a choice: to be radical but unacceptable; or to be cautious
and electable.
18 June 1994

*

To win the trust of the British people, we must do more than just
defeat the Conservatives on grounds of competence, integrity
and fitness to govern. We must change the tide of ideas.
Change and National Renewal, *23 June 1994*

*

I believe in politics that if you calculate too much, you miscal-
culate. Therefore there is no point in worrying. If it happens,
it happens, and if it doesn't, well, there's lots more to life.

People who become obsessive about political ambition usually are either a) dangerous or b) they fail.
Interview in The Times, *6 July 1994*

*

If people would stop thinking that you have to choose between saying nothing and being radical, but in a way that makes you entirely unelectable, then I think Labour could really move the whole of the left forward.
New Statesman, *15 July 1994*

*

I can't hope to replace the trust and affection in which the country held John [Smith]. I'm too young for that. I have to be something different. I have to be bold and exciting.
July 1994

*

I meant what I said about wanting to win power, not to enjoy it, but to change the country, to change its place in the world, to make it a country people are proud of again, to make this country of ours a country where everyone gets the chance to succeed and get on. We will win the next election, not by giving up our principles – that's not the business we're in – we're going to get power through principle, not at the expense of it. We will win, I am confident of that, but we will have to work for it. We will work for it, without any let-up, from this moment on. I've seen a lot of things over the past fifteen years that I've hated and loathed, and we've never been able to change them. I know that there exists within our party the discipline to make it happen.
Speech to Party colleagues on the day he won the Labour leadership, 21 July 1994

*

It is the confident who can change and the doubters who hesitate.
21 July 1994 (an unintended message for Gordon Brown?)

*

Much to the disgust of the Labour lefties, Tony Blair became the youngest ever Labour Party leader on 21 July. The never to be seen not smiling ex-public schoolboy pronounced triumphantly that he would not rest until his party was in its rightful place. Unfortunately, nobody was quite sure where that was.
From The Very Bloody History of Britain 2

*

I make no apology for having redefined the Labour Party's basic position on the economy, on welfare, on education, on a range of issues.
BBC Radio, 22 July 1994

*

So new politics is about a Stakeholder Democracy as well as a stakeholder economy. And that stake must also extend to the relationship between central government and the people.
John Smith Memorial Lecture, 7 February 1996

*

The Blairite revolution, converting Socialism into 'social-ism' and constructing a liberal communitarianism anchored in a broad intellectual inheritance of the left centre, succeeded

where the putative revisionism of a generation earlier had failed. The means and ends of socialism had finally been disentangled, not through evasion or obfuscation but through a direct and explicit process of theoretical reconstruction.
Dr Tony Wright MP, from Socialisms Old and New, *1996*

*

I do not believe you can build real and lasting trust just by telling people what they want to hear. Real trust is built by saying what we really mean to do.
Speech in Edinburgh, 28 June 1996

*

I believe we can be more ambitious in government if we are more sober and realistic in opposition.
Interview in the New Statesman, *July 1996*

Election '97

Now it's for real . . . I've prepared for this for a long time.
17 March 1997 – the day the election was called

*

This election is about trust. For that very reason we make a virtue of the fact that our manifesto does not promise the earth.
Manifesto Launch, 3 April 1997

*

Like any parish council.
Describing the spending powers of a Scottish Parliament, 4 April 1997

*

Put simply, he was not prepared to utter the words 'tax' and 'up' in the same sentence, however theoretical, because he knew his words would be twisted and used against him.
Daily Mirror *journalist John Williams, 4 April 1997*

*

This is where everything all began for me politically and where I have learned so much. I hope I have given something to this constituency party, but I have learned a lot here. I have seen decent people crying out for a different kind of Labour Party, that could rise above the problems of the past. I remember that 1983 election. John [Burton] stopped me watching the news because it made me so depressed. All the way through you kept faith in me. It was difficult because we were turning things over that people thought were cherished. You supported me all the way through and without you I could never have become leader of the Labour Party. It could never have happened because all the way through I had the foundation of my career solid here in Sedgefield. When I became leader I knew there was a place I could always come back to for some decent common sense. I remember all those years ago how we seemed to have lost our way and now we have found it.
Speech to his adoption meeting in Sedgefield, 4 April 1997

*

They have had three years to prepare their manifesto and in three days it's falling apart.
John Major, 6 April 1997

*

If I had stood for election on this platform and made the promises they [the Conservatives] made, I would not have the gall to ask the British people to trust me again. Yet this is what the Conservatives do today.
8 April 1997

*

They look all of twenty-two. That's one year for every Tory
tax rise.
Response to youthful heckling during the 1997 election campaign

*

Tony Blair is cracking under the strain.
Michael Heseltine, 8 April 1997

*

I can't stand the hypocrisy of a man who says that he would
deny the choice in the education system and then opts for
choice for his own children. A man that will do that is not fit
to discuss this country's education policy, let alone be Prime
Minister.
Michael Heseltine, 14 April 1997

*

The sun is out, and in two weeks so will the Tories be.
In Crawley, 15 April 1997

*

Even if you vote for a different party, do vote. People fought
long and hard for the right to vote. I have very little time for
people who say it makes no difference.
15 April 1997

*

They can't come back from this.
*On hearing that Tory Minister John Horam had broken ranks and declared
himself against a single currency, 15 April 1997*

*

You can't run a Party like this.
On the Tory disarray over Europe, 16 April 1997

*

There are two Conservative Parties fighting this election. I think neither will be elected.
16 April 1997

*

It will be a New Labour Government's task to rebuild Britain as one nation where every individual has a stake in its future, where we treat poverty and unemployment not as problems we shut out or ignore, but as intolerable in any decent society true to the best of British values.
16 April 1997

*

A decent society judges itself by the conditions of the weak as well as the strong.
16 April 1997

*

I want to be elected because I believe I can make this country better. I want to be elected because for eighteen years I have been a doer not a sayer and I came into politics to get things done.
16 April 1997

*

I am a British patriot. I will always put the interests of my country first. But the Britain of my vision is not a Britain turning its back on the world – narrow, shy, uncertain.
19 April 1997

*

I am a modern man, from the rock 'n' roll generation. The Beatles, colour TV, that's my generation.
20 April 1997

*

I really think we're going to do this.
22 April 1997

*

We approach these last few days with a sense of humility and a sense of responsibility, but a sense of excitement and hope as well.
27 April 1997

*

I think I have got less tense as the campaign has gone on. I know where I am going, and a compartment of my mind has been increasingly occupied with that.
April 1997

*

I don't believe this is a landslide country.
28 April 1997

*

Can I say a word of thanks to whoever put the posters up?
After a poster fell down behind him during a press conference, 28 April 1997

*

John Smith said the night before he died: 'All we ask is the chance to serve.'
29 April 1997

*

It would be odd if there wasn't a mild sense of anticipation. I don't think that would be overdoing it.
A tongue-in-cheek response to a reporter who asked if he would feel a sense of anticipation when the polls closed, 30 April 1997

*

You've no chance with any of those.
To Mirror *reporter John Williams who had drawn Labour majorities of 105, 115 and 129 in the journalists' election sweepstake, 30 April 1997*

*

The very simple choice that people have got in this next twenty-four hours is this. It is twenty-four hours to save the NHS, twenty-four hours to give our children the education they need, twenty-four hours to give hope to our young people, security to our elderly.
30 April 1997

*

You're having me on.
To aides who told him of the scale of the landslide, 2 May 1997

*

All that could make this complete was that my mother was here still.

Victory speech at the Sedgefield count, 2 May 1997

*

A new dawn has broken. Isn't it wonderful? We always said that if we had the courage to change we could do it and we did it. The British people have put their trust in us. It is a moving and humbling experience. The size of our majority places a special responsibility on us. We have been elected as New Labour and we will govern as New Labour. We were elected because as a party today we represent the whole of this nation, every single day. We will speak up for that decent, hardworking majority of the British people whose voices have been silent for too long and we will set about doing the good, practical things that need to be done – extending educational opportunity, not to an elite, but to all our children, modernizing our welfare state, rebuilding our National Health Service as a proper National Health Service. We will work with business to create the dynamic and enterprising economy we will need. We will work for all our people to create that just and decent society the British people have wanted for so long. This vote tonight has been a vote for the future, for a new era of politics in Britain. So let us put behind us the battles of this last century and address the new challenge of this new century, when we build a nation united, with no one shut out, no one excluded. That is the country we have wanted for so long, a country whose politics live up to the finest ideals of public service and a Britain that stands tall in the world, whose sense of its future is as certain and confident as its sense of its own history. We have won support in this election from all walks of life, all classes of people, every corner of our country. We are now today the people's party, the party of all the people, the many not the few, the party that belongs to every part of Britain. I want everyone to feel proud of their country tonight because everyone has a stake in its success. Tonight the people of Britain are uniting behind New Labour, they are uniting around decent British values, uniting to face the challenge of the future, uniting at long last as one nation. Three days ago I quoted John Smith. He said, 'All we ask is the chance to serve.' Tonight the British people have given us the chance to serve and serve we will with all our heart. We say tonight – you the British people have given us the chance to serve, you have put your trust in us. We say to you – we shall repay that trust. We have been people saying, but never given the chance to do and yet the only purpose of being in politics is to make things happen. Now we have the chance to make things happen. We take that responsibility upon us. We will discharge it and we shall make this country proud of us as tonight we are proud of them.

Speech to Labour supporters on election night at the Royal Festival Hall, 5.30am, 2 May 1997

*

I have received thousands of pieces of information from Tony Blair's office over the past few weeks but not one about what I am supposed to do now. I hope they send it soon.

Rudi Vis, the unexpectedly victorious Labour candidate in Finchley, 2 May 1997

*

In drei und siebzig Wochen machen wir es genauso. Herzlichen Glückwunsch, Tony Blair.

SPD Poster unveiled in Bonn, 2 May 1997 (In seventy-three weeks, we'll do it too. Congratulations Tony Blair)

*

The British people have put their faith in me. I will not let
them down.
Speaking following his victory in Sedgefield, 2 May 1997

*

If I can say this to Lizzy, I once fought a very hopeless seat,
Beaconsfield in the South – and look what happened to me!
*To his Tory opponent in Sedgefield Elizabeth Pitman, at the count on election
night, 2 May 1997*

*

I should like to begin by paying tribute to my predecessor
John Major, for his dignity and his courage over these last few
days and for the manner of his leaving, the essential decency
of which is the mark of the man.
First words on John Major outside Ten Downing Street, 2 May 1997

*

For eighteen long years my party has been in opposition. It
could only say, it could not do. Today we are charged with the
deep responsibility of government. Today, enough of talking,
it is time now to do.
On the steps of Number Ten, 2 May 1997

*

It will be a government rooted in strong values, the values of
justice and progress and community, the values that have
guided me all my political life. But a government ready with
the courage to embrace the new ideas necessary to make

those values live again for today's world.
2 May 1997

*

We are not the masters. The people are the masters. We are the people's servants.
Blair's first address to his 418 Labour MPs, 7 May 1997

*

What can he want?
On being told the Deputy Prime Minister wanted a word and immediately thinking it was Michael Heseltine, May 1997

*

We were elected as New Labour and we govern as New Labour.
At the first Cabinet meeting of the new Government, 8 May 1997

*

Don't underestimate the difference between government and opposition. The fact you can actually do things, take decisions affecting people's lives for the better is the best tonic you could ask for.
Quoted in the Sunday Times, *11 May 1997*

*

We speak as the One Nation party in British politics today. We speak for the whole nation and we will serve the whole nation.
Response to the Queen's Speech, Hansard, *15 May 1997*

*

Our mandate is clear: to modernize what is outdated; to make fair what is unjust; and to do both by the best means available, irrespective of dogma or doctrine, without fear or favour. And there is much to do.

Ibid.

Part Six

FRIENDS AND FOES

On Others

I'll say this once, and I won't say it again. I can never, ever repay you for what you've done for me.
To Sedgefield constituency agent John Burton following his victory, June 1983

*

He had this extraordinary combination of strength and authority and humour and humanity, and all of us who knew him closely, personally, will mourn him. I think the whole country will feel the loss, and our thoughts and prayers go out to Elizabeth and the family. But it's simply devastating.
Tribute to John Smith on BBC TV News, 12 May 1994

*

She's paying the price for trying to flit between left and right and has only herself to blame if she doesn't get either job.
On Margaret Beckett's decision to run for both the Leadership and Deputy Leadership of the Labour Party. Quoted in Tony Blair – The Modernizer *by Jon Sopel*

*

I met Anji when I was about seventeen, at a party where we

both stayed overnight. It was my first defeat.
On his long-time personal assistant Anji Hunter, 21 July 1994

*

It would be absurd of me to say that my views and Charles Kennedy's are a million miles apart. They're not.
Observer, *2 October 1994*

*

Commissioner Kinnock – a credit to our Party here, as he will be to our country in Brussels.
On Neil Kinnock's appointment as European Commissioner, Speech to Labour Party Conference, October 1994

*

I have an extremely good relationship with John Prescott . . . He is an enormous asset to the Party and I get on extremely well with him.
Daily Mirror, *26 January 1996*

*

And we have a better shadow cabinet, in my view, than we've had at any point in time, certainly in my experience, in terms of its stability and capability.
Independent, *13 July 1996*

*

I think that John Prescott will be a very big part of an incoming Labour government . . . I can assure you he will be a big player in that government.
BBC TV, 12 January 1997

*

He follows his party, I lead mine.
On John Major, February 1997

*

He has our tremendous respect and gratitude and support.
On Neil Kinnock after the 1992 defeat, April 1997

*

Look at the Tory Party, pause and reflect. And vow never to let us emulate them.
To Labour MPs, 7 May 1997

*

Let me congratulate you for the magnificent part you played in our victory.
To Tory Euro-sceptic MPs, Hansard, 14 May 1997

On the Enemy

The Right Honourable Gentleman takes the biscuit.
*To Michael Howard after he claimed the minimum wage would cost two
million jobs, July 1991*

*

I sit there in the House of Commons . . . sitting there opposite
me are people doing things . . . I have sat there and watched
those people ruin our country.
Speech to the TUC, 12 September 1995

*

That part of the Liberal Democrats that is essentially social
democratic has a lot in common with parts of the Labour
Party.
The Times, *18 September 1995*

*

There will be a lot of people who object to what I am saying.

But I think increased co-operation with the Liberal Democrats is sensible.
Ibid.

*

She came to confuse the notion of knowing your own mind with refusing to listen to anyone else. I do not admire that.
On Margaret Thatcher, Interview in The Times, *6 July 1994*

*

It was the clear sense of an identifiable project for the Tory Party that I did admire. It is absolutely essential in politics. That is what keeps you going.
On Margaret Thatcher, The Times, *6 July 1994*

*

The product of an unchecked and unbalanced mind.
On Margaret Thatcher's housing policies, June 1987

*

A lot of nonsense was talked about Thatcher being a great conviction politician.
The Spectator, *1 October 1994*

*

She was a thoroughly determined person and that is an admirable quality. It is important in politics to have a clear sense of direction, to know what you want. I believe I know what Britain needs.
On Margaret Thatcher, Sunday Times, *23 April 1995*

*

It has surely come to something when a government can only secure the passage of its own legislative programme by threatening its own demise.
On John Major's warning to Tory Eurosceptics, Independent, *17 November 1994*

*

The Conservative Party is a lie machine which is prepared to accuse us of anything regardless of the truth.
Speech to Welsh Labour Party Conference, 19 May 1995

*

There is nothing they will not try to get re-elected. No policy they won't overturn. No trick they are not prepared to pull.
Ibid.

*

The New Right asked some of the right questions in the 1980s about how we could be more enterprising as a nation. In the end it was a project more successful at destroying than creating.
Renewal, *4 October 1995*

*

Sleaze has become the hallmark of the dying days of this administration.
Speech to Time Magazine *Dinner, 30 November 1995*

*

What is clear is that the Tory Lie Machine has moved up a

gear as the election nears. But we have seen nothing yet. They will smear, as they always do, and lie and cheat and spend vast sums on untruthful propaganda.
Speech to Scottish Labour Party Dinner, 8 December 1995

*

The Conservatives want to turn their fire on Labour, they are going to engage in a series of the most wild and personal attacks.
BBC Radio, 29 January 1996

*

What we have governing our country is a degenerate party that loves lecturing people about right and wrong but has long since ceased to know the difference between right and wrong itself.
Speech in Swansea, 10 May 1996

Friends of Tony

Even before he became an MP and famous I always thought of Tony as the only 'nice' person that I ever went out with at Oxford. He was very good looking, in a kind of sweet way, and wasn't all that predatory. He was very different from most of the guys I knew, but I guess I fell for him because he was cute.

Blair's Oxford girlfriend, American Mary Harron, quoted in Tony Blair – The Modernizer *by Jon Sopel*

*

In my view Tony Blair will make a major contribution to British politics in the months and years ahead.

Michael Foot, BBC TV, 26 May 1982

*

A very big future in British politics.

Roy Hattersley, BBC TV Newsnight *following Blair's defeat in the 1983 Beaconsfield by-election*

*

We've got to support him, you know. He's Cabinet material.
Sedgefield Labour Party Agent John Burton prior to Blair's selection as Parliamentary Candidate, May 1983

*

Not another fucking Labour barrister.
Greg Dyke, on being introduced to Tony Blair

*

The more you hear him attacked the more you must cherish him, because he's in for a terrible time over the next decade, because he's so good, and if you're good in this game, that's when they want to get you down.
Neil Kinnock to Blair's constituency party, May 1993 (quoted in John Rentoul's biography of Blair)

*

If you have given him a tricky job to do and he has put his mind to it, you'll see that he will do it brilliantly. He does not do it effortlessly, but he does it brilliantly. When people say he is shallow, they haven't understood him at all. He has worked hard at ideas, just as he worked hard mastering complicated briefs.
Maggie Rae interviewed in Andy McSmith's Faces of Labour

*

If you decide you want to be leader of the party, you will be leader.
David Blunkett, May 1994

*

The ministerial Rovers are coming whether we like it or not.
Tony Wright MP to Tony Blair, May 1994 (Blair left him out of his Ministerial team when the time came)

*

Blair applies himself to every problem with a steady and determined intelligence, without the flashy and erratic brilliance often found in the precociously successful. All the tasks that a modern politician is required to do, Blair does well.
Andy McSmith, Faces of Labour, *1994*

*

I had quite fundamental disagreements with Tony.
John Prescott, 25 June 1994

*

I do not agree with many of his views, quite frankly.
John Prescott on Tony Blair, The Times, 29 June 1994

*

He was absolutely excellent. I have no doubt that he would have become a QC. He had a very keen sense of what was relevant. He was very good at getting to the point. He was a fast gun on paper, possessing an excellent facility with the English language.
Lord Irvine of Lairg on Blair the lawyer, Sunday Times, 17 July 1994

*

This man, our new leader, has got what it takes. He

commands moral authority and political respect. He has the energy and vitality to win people over to Labour . . . and he scares the life out of the Tories. And me!
John Prescott, 21 July 1994

*

He is charming without being charismatic, engaging without being warm. He inspires loyalty in those with whom he has worked. He consults widely, but partly as a tactic. He makes quick and firm decisions when he has to, but will avoid them until a deadline looms. He is an immensely cautious risk-taker.
John Rentoul, Tony Blair's biographer

*

Few politicians are good at taking the high ground and throwing themselves off it. Tony does it, and takes enormous care to bring everyone else with him. He manages the process of risk-taking with great appreciation to detail.
Peter Mandelson, New Yorker, 5 February 1996

*

He [Tony Blair] should talk more about what we stand for and . . . there should be less modifying everything we stand for . . . I think the obsession with the media and the focus groups is making us look as if we want power at any price.
Clare Short, New Statesman, 9 August 1996

*

Tony's advisers . . . I sometimes call them the people who live in the dark. Everything they do is in hiding.
Ibid.

*

The chances of Tony Blair asking me to do anything other
than shut up and vote are extremely remote.
*Tony Banks MP, February 1997. Three months later Blair appointed him
Minister for Sport*

*

Someone who can fight the buggers on their own terms.
Barbara Castle, March 1997

*

Tony Blair asked the British people to trust him and he deserves
at least a couple of years to prove himself worthy of that.
Richard Branson, 2 May 1997

*

As a fellow junior frontbencher Tony Blair advised me when
I had my first question number one. He told me to spend the
whole morning preparing it. 'Forget the mail, forget tele-
phone calls. Work on the question.'
Paul Flynn MP, May 1997

*

That's the way things go. You've just got to keep going and be
decent in your relations with people. You never know what's
going to happen in the future.
Gordon Brown on his decision to allow Tony Blair a free run at the leadership,
Sunday Times, *11 May 1997*

*

Based on conversations I've had with him and the fast start he has made, we have a chance to have a very good partnership.
President Clinton, Observer, *25 May 1997*

*

You have good eyes, a bright mind, the right age and good experience. Great Britain is in good hands.
President Boris Yeltsin, 27 May 1997

*

With Tony you have to learn to take the smooth with the smooth.
Anonymous senior Labour politician on his leader

Enemies of Tony

Too nice and too unguarded to be a politician.
Godfrey Barker, Daily Telegraph, *May 1982*

*

He will bring an economic literacy, ability and good humour
that has been sadly lacking from the opposition front bench.
Nicholas Soames MP, Hansard, *20 July 1987*

*

He's a very effective parliamentary performer. He doesn't
speak for the sake of speaking . . . He asks very pointed questions. I did once take the Finance Bill through committee
when he was my opposite number and I was very impressed
a) by how much he's done his homework, and b) by his ability to think quickly on his feet.
Norman Lamont, BBC TV, November 1988

*

As Blair and his impertinent young political pups wage war

on old Labour ... as they seek to kill off their fathers, these political adolescents boost themselves with a dangerous amnesic and, thus drugged, the courageous volunteers, manned with piss-proud erections, dare to obliterate the reality that the most radical and 'regenerative Labour government', that brought us the welfare state, was led by old men.

Leo Abse

*

As actor or performer doubtless Blair brought pleasure; his small step from stage to political platform in search of identity may have assisted him in his personal resolution, but it left my Labour Party shorn; he has taken away the identity of Labour and reshaped it to suit his own psychological measurements. This operation is described by his supporters as 'reform'. I call it theft ... Rock on Blair, with the moondust and with the kids. But count me and Old Labour out.

Leo Abse

*

[Tony Blair's] views on the European Community are indistinguishable from my own.

Kenneth Clarke, Hansard, 1 February 1993

*

I find myself in complete agreement with somebody like Tony Blair and his stress on social cohesion and community values.

Chris Patten, Sunday Times, 10 April 1994

*

Why should you believe a man who has got all the major

judgements wrong in the first half of his life, when he tells you
he is going to get them all right in the second half of his life?
Michael Heseltine, BBC Radio, 15 September 1994

*

He is quite stoically bland. The sheer blandness is so totally
inherent that it is quite difficult to embarrass him. He will
cope with the party because I don't think anyone will launch
an attack on him, at least until he's Prime Minister. After he is
Prime Minister, I think the whole thing will change. Then he
will have a lot of problems in the Labour Party.
Brian Sedgemore MP, Faces of Labour, *1994*

*

The Conservative government faces a monumental challenge
from the new and fresh leadership of Tony Blair. It can hardly
be overestimated. Blair has moved the party sharply to the
centre.
Norman Lamont, Daily Mail, *8 November 1994*

*

He had first come to my notice at the time of the leadership
election (in 1983). A meeting of Peter Shore supporters had
been called and I remember being gratified to see at that small
gathering a young newcomer. We did not see him again at
such a meeting; it was only later that I realized he had gone to
every candidate's campaign meeting, rather as an Oxford
fresher might join each political club.
Bryan Gould, from Goodbye to All That, *1995*

*

He is, quite simply, a Liberal . . . This young man has not the

faintest idea of how socialists think and does not begin to understand the mentality of the party he has been elected to lead.
Ken Coates MEP, Daily Telegraph, *13 January 1995*

*

It is undeniably true that without Neil Kinnock, there could have been no Tony Blair.
Steven Norris, from Changing Trains, *October 1996*

*

I cannot ignore the clear evidence that the next Labour government will not be composed of a near set of Blair clones. Were it to be I could live with it, except that Tony is a shade too right wing for me on some issues, but when a party decides to hold its nose and think of victory, to allow its leader to mouth whatever platitudes are necessary to obtain power, then beware what will follow.
Ibid.

*

His speeches often consist almost entirely of 'mood music' with some rather grandiose assertions mixed in.
David Willetts MP, June 1996

*

Tony Blair's position as leader of the Labour Party is weaker than that of any leader in memory ... He is unaware of just how widespread is the dissatisfaction and outright anger at the style of his leadership and policies among those MPs who put him in the leadership.
Cassandra, anonymous Labour MP in a Tribune *article, 15 November 1996*

*

What makes Tony Blair so dangerous for us is that people could vote for him and forget they're voting Labour.
Anonymous Tory backbencher quoted in Tony Blair – The Modernizer *by Jon Sopel*

*

If Blair turns out to be as good as he looks we have a problem.
Tory Party Deputy Chairman John Maples in a leaked strategy memo

*

A numbing fusillade of platitudes ... his brain permanently on line to a fad lexicon ... Mr Blair uses abstract nouns as a wine writer uses adjectives, filling space with a frothy concoction devoid of meaning.
Simon Jenkins, Former Editor of The Times

*

The trouble is that he is Bill Clinton with his flies done up.
Anonymous Tory Minister quoted in Tony Blair – The Modernizer *by Jon Sopel*

*

He is probably the most formidable leader we have seen since Gaitskell. I see a lot of Socialism behind their front bench but not in Mr Blair – I think he has genuinely moved.
Margaret Thatcher, BBC TV, 1994

*

He says he believes in the things he is advocating and I

believe he does.
Margaret Thatcher, Interview in the Sunday Times, *28 June 1995*

*

He won't let Britain down.
Attributed to Margaret Thatcher, The Times, *14 March 1997*

*

Mr Blair is chicken.
Conservative Party Chairman, Dr Brian Mawhinney following Blair's refusal to take part in a TV debate with John Major, 3 April 1997

*

Terribly formal and rather unlived in.
Charlotte Atkins, Editor of House Beautiful *on the Blairs' home, quoted in* Yes Magazine, *27 April 1997*

*

The road to hell is paved with good intentions.
John Major on Labour's first Queen's Speech, 15 May 1997

*

The new government deserves some goodwill and it deserves some luck. I am willing to give it goodwill and for the sake of the country, I am prepared to wish it luck. No government has ever come to office with such an inheritance, but it was an inheritance won against daily opposition and obstruction of many of the members now sitting on the government benches.
John Major, Hansard, 15 May 1997

*

Blair's first mistake has been to make Peter Mandelson Minister Without Portfolio – with a career mistake by Mandelson in accepting it.

Lord Rodgers, New Statesman, *16 May 1997*

The Fourth Estate

Our news today is instant, hostile to subtlety or qualification. If you can't sum it up in a sentence, or even a phrase, forget it. Combine two ideas or sentiments together and mass communication will not repeat them. To avoid misinterpretation, strip down a policy or opinion to one key clear line before the media does it for you. Think in headlines.

Tony Blair, writing in The Times, *24·November 1987*

*

The Man Labour Missed.

Headline to a Sunday Times *colour supplement profile of Blair by Barbara Amiel, 19 July 1992 (the day following John Smith's election as Party leader)*

*

The only member of the Labour Party a normal person could ever vote for.

Private Eye, *1 January 1993*

*

The succession is decided. The heir is chosen. Step forward Tony Blair. Give way Gordon Brown.

Toby Helm, Sunday Telegraph, *28 February 1993*

*

Well dressed, well spoken, good looking and immensely plausible, [Blair] is just the sort of smoothie to lull the British public into forgetting that they are playing with fire ... Charmers like this must be denied the oxygen of publicity.

Matthew Parris, The Times, *11 March 1993*

*

If Roy Jenkins appeared to be trying to cup the breasts of young peasant girls, Tony Blair looks as if he were trying to stop him.

Simon Hoggart, Guardian, *6 July 1994*

*

Never, even in Islington, have so many generalities been uttered with such passion by a single politician within one lunchtime.

Matthew Parris on a Blair lunchtime address, 22 July 1994

*

Tony Blair scooped the Labour Party in his strong arms ... gazed long into eyes like amber pools of light, and told it how deeply he cared. Then, almost before the party knew what was happening, he led it, softly yet insistently towards the bedroom door.

Simon Hoggart, Guardian, *5 October 1994*

*

He sounded precise, rehearsed and a little tense – like a middle-ranking barrister with a good mind, a sharp tongue and a careful knowledge of his brief on his first important case; skilled enough to get it right, not quite relaxed enough to swing the big punch.

Matthew Parris on Tony Blair's first Prime Minister's Question Time perform-ance following his election as Party Leader, The Times, *19 October 1994*

*

Mr Blair drove at gathering velocity round a track littered with the death traps of policy commitments, swerving to avoid every one, fuelled by a tankful of abstract nouns.

Matthew Parris on Tony Blair's speech-making style

*

As so often in a Blair speech, as it progressed, it began to shed verbs. Sentences were reduced to a cluster. Nouns and pronouns. Sentences, verbless. 'Fairness at work. Practical proposals. In crime, tough on crime, tough on the causes of crime. In Europe, leadership not isolation . . .' In every area policy is New Labour. (Sorry, that does contain a verb, but sounds as if it doesn't.) Smaller classes. Shorter waiting lists. A turning point in British politics. New Labour. New Life for Britain. For too long, the party's energy wasted. On verbs. For the British people, now, no more verbs. Tough on verbs, tough on the causes of verbs. New Labour. New nouns, adjectives. Real words. Words for a new Britain. There is a purpose to this. Verbless sentences sound as if they are firm promises. The mind supplies the missing phrases: 'We shall provide . . . we will legislate for . . .' Yet nothing concrete has been proposed. Like so much of the manifesto, each verbless

phrase offers a fine aspiration, worthy in every way, utterly estimable, entirely vague.
Simon Hoggart on Tony Blair's speech introducing The Road to the Manifesto *policy document, 5 July 1996*

*

Blair sometimes gives the impression of having got a 'Be a Leader of the Opposition' kit for Christmas, painstakingly cutting along the dotted lines, working out which tabs have to be folded back and glued.
Matthew Parris, The Times, *20 November 1996*

*

The press is a tiger, and whether you like it or not, in politics you are put astride it but it is a pretty fearsome beast.
Desert Island Discs, *23 November 1996*

*

The book's going to be all right then.
To Daily Mirror *journalist John Williams, 1 May 1997. Williams planned a book on the election campaign called* Victory. *It depended on Labour winning.*

*

One day, when we have grown used to thinking of 1997 as earlier generations thought of 1945, it will be hard to recall how little we expected Blair's earthquake. I am convinced that he certainly didn't. Like all veterans of the 1992 Labour defeat, he was determined not to be deluded again. He set out expecting to win, but knowing it might yet go wrong. He was sure of victory in the second half of the campaign, but could not bring himself to believe that the huge poll

leads were right.
John Williams, Political Correspondent of the Daily Mirror, *3 May 1997*

*

Mr Blair is a man of rare ability. Rarer still in modern politics, he has an unblemished reputation for honesty and integrity that commands the respect even of his most committed opponents . . . Blair is a devoted and active father, practically rather than theoretically committed to family values.
Simon Heffer, Daily Mail, *13 May 1997*

*

Unreconstructed wankers.
Blair's description of the Scottish media, Independent on Sunday, *25 May 1997*

*

Now what lessons might Cherie have learned from her guest [Hilary Clinton]? Don't give up your day job. Never give an interview. Gaze adoringly at your husband on all occasions, but zip your lip. Don't parade your children. And don't try your hand at reorganizing the NHS on your own.
Polly Toynbee, Independent, *30 May 1997, following the Clintons' visit to Number Ten*

Part Seven

BUT SERIOUSLY…

Flip-Flops

All politicians change their minds. Some are more honest about it than others. Margaret Thatcher would deny until she was blue in the face that she had ever done a U-turn on any policy. In order to become electable, New Labour have had to perform some political acrobatics which make the term U-turn almost an understatement. So what? If you change your mind and come up with the right answer, it doesn't really matter how much your opponents chide you for it. The term 'flip-flop', apart from being a less than fetching form of footwear has also entered the political vocabulary in America. It was used to good effect by the Republicans against Bill Clinton in a TV advert which demonstrated how many times Bill Clinton has changed his policies in his first term as President. Roll the film . . .

*

Flip:
Without an active, interventionist industrial policy . . . Britain faces the future of having to compete on dangerously unequal terms.
The Times, *19 May 1988*

Flop:
New Labour does not believe it is the job of government to interfere in the running of business.
Speech to the Nottingham Chamber of Commerce, 19 January 1996

*

Flip:
I am absolutely committed to the goal of full employment.
Speech to Labour Party Conference, October 1994

Flop:
There is no longer such a thing as a job for life. Long-term structural unemployment has become a fact of life.
Speech in Cape Town, 14 October 1996

*

Flip:
We'll create two million jobs in five years.
1983 Election Address

Flop:
I don't actually favour putting targets on it [full employment].
BBC TV, 12 June 1994

*

Flip:
I agree entirely that if you set it [the minimum wage] too high it will have an adverse impact on the jobs market.
BBC TV Money Programme, *24 September 1995*

Flop:
I have not accepted that the minimum wage will cost jobs . . .

I have simply accepted that econometric models indicate a potential jobs impact.

Letter to the Independent

*

Flip:

Most people would accept that an employer gains if a trade union is weakened. The proposed form of electoral procedure imposed and enforced upon every trade union will enmesh trade unions in legal battles and cause them administrative obstacles. That will weaken their ability to pursue the industrial interest of their members.

Hansard, *26 March 1984*

Flop:

We are not going back to the old battles. You have heard me say this many times: I will say it again. There is not going to be a repeal of all Tory trade union laws. It is not what the members want – it is not what the country wants.

Speech to the TUC, 12 September 1995

*

Flip:

Under my leadership I will never allow this country to be isolated or left behind in Europe.

Speech to Labour Party Conference, 4 October 1994

Flop:

If it is in Britain's interests to be isolated through the use of the national veto, then we will be isolated.

*

Flip:
We'll negotiate a withdrawal from the EEC which has drained our natural resources and destroyed jobs.
Election Address in the 1983 General Election

Flop:
I always believed that it was important for Britain to be in Europe.
December 1994

*

Flip:
Having fought long and hard for [their freedoms, unions] will not give them up lightly ... We shall oppose the Bill which is a scandalous and undemocratic measure against the trade union movement.
Speaking on the Trade Union Bill, November 1983

Flop:
The basic elements of that legislation: ballots before strikes, for union elections [and] restrictions on mass picketing are here to stay.
November 1994

*

Flip:
Parliamentary Labour CND supports the removal of all nuclear weapons from British territory and expresses its solidarity with all campaigners for peace.
Text of a newspaper advert in Sanity *signed by Tony Blair in May 1986*

Flop:
Labour will retain Britain's nuclear capability, with the number of warheads no greater than the present total.
April 1992

*

Flip:
Labour is committed to a regional assembly for Wales and to regional assembles for England.
June 1994

Flop:
There is not a consensus about regional assemblies in England ... We are not committed to regional assemblies in England.
March 1995

Tony Blair's Vows

At the 1996 Labour Party Conference Tony Blair made ten vows to the Nation by which he wished to be judged by the end of a Labour Government's first term.

1. I vow that we will have increased the proportion of our national income we spend on education
2. I vow that we will have reduced the proportion we spend on welfare bills and social failure
3. I vow that we will have reduced the spending on NHS bureaucracy and increased it on patient care
4. I vow that we will have cut the number of long-term unemployed and cut by over a half the number of young people unemployed
5. I vow that we will have halved the time it takes for young offenders to get to court
6. I vow that we will keep the Government borrowing and inflation within the low and prudent targets we set within the economic cycle
7. I vow that the promises we make on tax we will keep
8. I vow that class sizes will be down in primary schools and standards up in all schools
9. I vow that with the consent of the people we will have

devolved power to Scotland, Wales and the regions of England

10. I vow that we will have built a new and constructive relationship in Europe

Twenty Examples of Blair Blah

Meaningless phrases with good alliteration and very few verbs. That's what Blair blah is all about. For those not familiar with the term, I first heard it used in Norfolk by a redoubtable lady called Marjorie Lloyd, who would listen attentively to a political speech and then dismiss it with the words: 'Doesn't mean a thing – it's all blah!' Tony Blair's skill is that he mixes blah with substance. But he does have a tendency to overdo it, play to the crowd. New Labour New Britain. Britain united. One Nation. New Labour. See what I mean?

1. The power of all for the good of each
2. Ours is a passion allied to reason
3. A thousand days for a thousand years
4. Labour's coming home
5. Tough on crime – tough on the causes of crime
6. Saying what we mean, meaning what we say
7. A hand up, not a hand out
8. Using the power of all for the good of each
9. Long-termism in action
10. Education, Education, Education
11. Call me Tony
12. The settlement train is leaving
13. Marching in step to a General Election

14. Let us say what we mean and mean what we say
15. Fairness, not favours
16. Education is liberty
17. Nation of all the talents
18. Leadership not drift
19. For the many not the few
20. For the future, not the past

Twenty-Seven Things You Didn't Know About Tony Blair

(Courtesy of Matthew Parris)

1. He has terrible teeth.
2. He looks like a vampire.
3. It is not true that Tony Blair is attractive to women. He's too pretty. He's a man's idea of a man who attracts women. Seven out of nine women in the Westminster Press Gallery do not fancy Tony Blair. Gordon Brown scores four.
4. He went to public school.
5. He went to Oxford.
6. His dad became a Tory.
7. He smiles too much.
8. He cannot possibly be as nice as he seems. All politicians must rise through a nasty political process, work with nasty people in nasty parties and prosper. He has. He must be pretending to be nice.
9. He cannot lack a simple ambition for office as he claims. He must be lying.
10. He has never held down any job in Government.
11. He spends too much time on his hair.
12. He looks like a prototype for something, but nobody is sure what.

13. Nobody had heard of him before 1992.
14. He may be a Vulcan. This man is too good to be true. I believe that military strategists on the planet Vulcan, having infiltrated into Westminster an early attempt at an Earthling politician, John Redwood, have now learnt from the mistakes in this design. They have sent an improved version with added charm. He has pointed ears.
15. He probably approves of Cliff Richard.
16. He may be Cliff Richard.
17. The Tories will say he's a boy sent to do a man's job.
18. Richard Littlejohn supports him.
19. He used to wear flares.
20. He was almost certainly a fan of Peter, Paul and Mary; the New Seekers; the Carpenters; Bucks Fizz; Abba...
21. He probably listens to Classic FM now.
22. His father was a lawyer.
23. He could just as well have been the leader of the Conservative Party or the SDP or the Liberal Party or the Green Party or Archbishop of Canterbury or a progressive missionary, or in charge of Bob Geldof's PR, or director of a major charity, or chairman of English Heritage, or General Secretary of a small, service sector trade union, or a management consultant, or King Herod, or the leader of the Dutch Social Democrats, or manager of a small plastics factory in Enfield where he is also sidesman in the local church and takes his daughter to pony classes in a newish Volvo.
24. He wears pastel suits.
25. He reminds us of Bill Clinton.
26. If he had ever smoked marijuana he would not have inhaled.
27. He doesn't fool me.

Tony Blair's ABC

In his *Times* column, Matthew Parris devised an ABC Guide
to Blair-speak. He wrote in July 1994: 'Labour MPs hoping for
a job under the new leader would be wise to draw their
speeches and their tone from this lexicon. Get ahead of the
pack: get in tune with Tony now.' As ever, Matthew was
ahead of his time . . .

*

A is for Achievement. Achievements are one of the main
things a Blair government will achieve. A is also for Abstract.
Abstract nouns are another Blair achievement. A is for
Absolutely, too. 'Absolutely' means 'yes' in Islington.

*

B is for Beliefs. Politics is about beliefs. B is for Basic. Basic
beliefs. B is for Broader society. And B is for the Battle of Ideas:
'Only by re-establishing its core identity can the Labour Party
regain the intellectual self-confidence to take on and win the
Battle of Ideas'. (*Fabian*/Guardian *Conference, 18 June 1994*)

*

C is for Core Identity; also Core beliefs; also Community, Citizenship, Cohesion, Compassion, Confidence, Coalition and Change.

*

D is for Duty: 'Individuals owe a Duty to one another and to a broader society.' (ibid.) D is also for Direction, new Direction, and Drive in a new direction.

*

E is for Energy: 'The power and Energy of ideas and vision.' (ibid.) E is for Equality, too 'Social justice. Cohesion, Equality of opportunity and community.' (ibid.) and for Ethical Socialism, as distinguished from unethical socialism.

*

F is for Fairness, for Freedom and for Full employability.

*

G is for Global: 'First, the economy is Global.' (ibid.) Labour's foreign and defence policy are also likely to be Global.

*

H is for Historic mission. Also for Historic opportunity: 'A Historic opportunity now to give leadership.' (ibid.)

*

I is for Initiative. No minister will be without one. As well as

Initiatives, a Blair administration will have Ideas: 'The future will be decided . . . through the power and energy of Ideas and vision.' (ibid.)

*

J is for Justice and social Justice (see Ethical Socialism).

*

K is for Key values and also for key beliefs (see also Core values and Core beliefs): 'Socialism as defined by certain Key values and beliefs is not merely alive, it has a historic opportunity now to give Leadership.' (ibid.)

*

L is for Leadership (see Historic opportunity/Key values).

*

M is for Modern: 'A future that is both radical and Modern.' (ibid.) M is for Movement, too: 'A radical Movement in this country for change and national renewal.' (ibid.)

*

N is for National renewal.

*

O is for Opportunity: '. . . the chance to capture the entire ground and language of Opportunity.' (ibid.) (See Equality.)

*

P is for Partnership. P is also for Purpose, Power, Potential and Pluralism: 'A greater Pluralism of ideas and thought.' (ibid.) (See also Ideas and Thought).

*

Q is for Quality work: 'Central to my belief about this country is that we've got to give people the chance not to work, but actually to have Quality work.' (*Interview with David Frost, 12 June 1994*)

*

R is for Rediscovery, Responsibilities, Realization and Respect: 'We do need to Rediscover a strong sense of civic and community values, the belief that we must combine opportunities and Responsibilities, and the Realization that true self-respect can come only through respect for others.' (*Speech to the CBI, 14 June 1994*)

*

S is for Society; and plural Society, and shared Society, and broader Society, and changed Society, and Social ... and 'Social-*ism*' – if you will.' (*Fabian*/Guardian *speech*)

*

T is for Tough: 'Tough on crime, Tough on the causes of crime.' T is also for Thinking, Thought, Trust and True self-respect.

*

U is for Urgency. (ibid.) U is also for United: 'A strong, United society which gives each citizen the chance to develop their potential to the full.' (ibid.) (See also Society and Potential.)

*

V is for Values. For Vigour and Victory too; and, more than all else, V is for Vision: '. . . A central Vision based around principle but liberated from particular policy prescriptions . . .' (ibid.) You can say that again!

*

W is for Worth: 'The equal Worth of each citizen.' (ibid.) W is also for Welfare and Well-being.

*

X is for X factor. John Major doesn't have it, according to a survey conducted for Mazda cars. Tony Blair has Factor X.

*

Y is for Youth. Blair has that, too.

*

Z is for Zero-sum game. A Zero-sum game is a calculation in which if you add to one thing you must take it away from another. Blair's economics, as he has said, is not a Zero-sum game. This means that you can have your cake and eat it.

Blair's Buzzwords

Following hot on the heels of Blair Blah are Blair Buzzwords. They feature in virtually every Blair speech. They figure prominently in this book. The word 'new' figures 111 times in this book. Socialism gets ten mentions.

Achievement
Change
Community
Energy
Fairness
Freedom
Ideas
New
Opportunity
Partnership
Radical
Responsibility
Stakehold
Socialism
Tough
Trust
Truth
Value

Blair Cheek!

A politician who is given a nickname has made it. The higher up the greasy pole of politics you get, the more nicknames are given to you – mostly of a fairly insulting nature. So far, Tony Blair has escaped fairly lightly. Here are my top ten . . .

Anagram of Tony Blair MP: I'm Tory Plan B (Text of a postcard by Gathered Images)
All mouth and no trousers (Michael Mansfield QC)
Bambi
Boy Wonder
Chicken Blair
Phoney Tony
Stalin
Tony Blur
Tory Blair
Tabloid Politician (Ken Clarke)

Tony Blair's Desert Island Discs

In November 1996 Tony Blair was granted an audience with Sue Lawley on Radio Four's long-running series, *Desert Island Discs*. Blair's choice of records to take with him to his mythical island would be typical of many of his generation. The group Etio became famous overnight, following his choice of their song 'Cancel Today'. Little has been heard of them since.

'Cancel Today' by Etio
'Clair de Lune' by Debussy
'In my Life' by The Beatles
'Fourth of July, Asprey Park' by Bruce Springsteen
Theme from *Platoon*
'Crossroad Blues' by Robert Johnson
'Wishing Well' by Free
'Memories of the Alhambra' by John Williams
Book: *Ivanhoe* by Walter Scott
Luxury Item: Guitar

Appendix 1

Career Chronology

Full Name:	Anthony Charles Lynton Blair
Born:	6 May 1953
Education:	1964–71, Fettes School, Edinburgh
	1972–75, St John's College, Oxford

Married to Cherie Booth, 29 March 1980

Children:	Euan
	Nicholas
	Kathryn

Sponsoring Trade Union: Transport & General Workers

1975–76	Student at Inns of Court, London
1976–77	Pupil at Chambers of Alexander (Derry) Irvine QC
1977–83	Lawyer specializing in industrial relations and employment law
May 1982	Labour candidate in Beaconsfield by-election
May 1983	Selected as prospective parliamentary candidate for Sedgefield
June 1983	Elected to the House of Commons as MP for Sedgefield with a majority of 8,281

November 1984	Appointed to the Labour Treasury team under Roy Hattersley
June 1987	Wins Sedgefield at the General Election
November 1987	Came seventeenth in Shadow Cabinet Elections with eighty-eight votes and promoted to Opposition Spokesman on Trade and Industry
November 1988	Elected to the Shadow Cabinet as Shadow Energy Secretary with 111 votes
November 1989	Reshuffled to be Shadow Employment Secretary
April 1992	Wins Sedgefield again at the General Election
November 1992	Appointed Shadow Home Secretary
November 1992	Elected to the National Executive Committee of the Labour Party
June 1994	Announces candidacy for Party Leadership, following John Smith's death in May
21 July 1994	Elected Leader of the Labour Party
October 1994	Announces review of Clause IV of the Labour Party constitution
1 May 1997	Leads Labour to a landslide victory in the General Election
2 May 1997	Announces first Cabinet appointments

Appendix 2

The Blair Essentials – Further Reading

Understanding where Tony Blair has come from and the ideas which have contributed to his thinking and beliefs is no easy task. But the student of Blairism (if such a thing exists) is not entirely without help. A multitude of books have been published in the last five years on the metamorphosis of the Labour Party from Old Labour to New Labour. Listed below are some of the more important volumes together with a range of other books which put the Blair victory into an historical context.

Abse, Leo — *The Man Behind the Smile – Tony Blair and the Politics of Perversion* (Robson Books, 1996)

Barratt Brown, Michael and Ken Coates — *Blair Revelation – Deliverance from whom?* (Spokesman, 1996)

Blair, Tony	*New Britain – My Vision of a Young Country* (Fourth Estate, 1996)
Brown, Gordon	*Values, Visions and Voices* (Mainstream, 1995)
Butler, Anthony	*The Future of Socialism in Western Europe* (Macmillan, 1997)
Coates, Ken	*New Labour's Aims and Values – A Study in Ambiguity* (ELP, 1996)
Coopey, R (ed.) *et al.*	*The Wilson Governments 1964–70* (Pinter, 1993)
Desai, Radhika	*Intellectuals and Socialism* (Lawrence & Wishart, 1994)
Duncan, Alan	*Beware Blair!* (Conservative Central Office, 1997)
Fielding, Steven	*The Labour Party: Socialism and Society Since 1951* (Manchester, 1997)
Foote, Geoffrey	*Labour Party's Political Thought – A History* (Macmillan, 1997)
Hain, Peter	*Ayes to the Left: A Future for Socialism* (Lawrence & Wishart, 1995)
Jeffreys, Kevin	*The Labour Party Since 1945* (Macmillan, 1993)
Jones, Tudor	*Remaking the Labour Party* (Routledge, 1996)
Layard, Richard	*What Labour Can Do* (Warner, 1997)
Laybourn, Keith	*The Rise of Socialism in Britain* (Sutton, 1996)
Mandelson, Peter and Roger Liddle	*The Blair Revolution – Can New Labour Deliver?* (Faber & Faber, 1996)
McKinstrey, Leo	*Fit to Govern?* (Bantam, 1996)
McSmith, Andy	*Faces of Labour* (Verso, 1996)
Miliband, David	*Reinventing the Left* (Polity, 1994)
Mitchell, Austin	*Last Time: Labour's Lessons from the Sixties* (Bellew, 1997)

Pelling, Henry
and Alastair Reid   *A Short History of the Labour Party* (Macmillan, 1996)

Perryman, Mark   *The Blair Agenda* (Lawrence & Wishart, 1996)

Plender, John   *A Stake in the Future – The Stakeholding Solution* (Nicholas Brealey, 1997)

Radice, Giles   *What Needs to Change – New Visions for Britain* (HarperCollins, 1996)

Rentoul, John   *Tony Blair* (Warner, 1996)

Sassoon, Donald   *One Hundred Years of Socialism* (I B Tauris, 1996)

Scruton, Roger   *Thinkers of the New Left* (Longman, 1985)

Shaw, Eric   *Labour Party Since 1979* (Routledge, 1994)

——   *Labour Party Since 1945* (Blackwell, 1996)

Smith, John   *Reclaiming the Ground – Christianity and Socialism* (Spire, 1993)

Sopel, Jon   *Tony Blair – The Modernizer* (Michael Joseph, 1995)

Taylor, Gerald   *Labour's Renewal – The Policy Review and Beyond* (Macmillan, 1997)

Thompson, Noel   *Political Economy and the Labour Party* (UCL Press, 1996)

Thompson, Willie   *Long Death of British Labourism* (Pluto, 1993)

Thorpe, Andrew   *History of the British Labour Party* (Macmillan, 1997)

Weinbren, Daniel   *Generating Socialism – Recollections of Life in the Labour Party* (Sutton, 1997)

Wickham-Jones,
Mark   *Economic Strategy and the Labour Party* (Macmillan, 1996)

Willetts, David   *Blair's Gurus* (Centre for Policy Studies, 1996)

Williams, John   *Victory – With Tony Blair on the Road to a Landslide* (Buchman, 1997)

Wright, Tony   *Socialisms Old and New* (Routledge, 1996)

——   *People's Party* (Thames & Hudson, 1997)

——   *Why Vote Labour?* (Penguin, 1997)

Bibliography

Abse, Leo	*The Man Behind the Smile – Tony Blair and the Politics of Perversion* (Robson Books, 1996)
Blair, Tony	*New Britain – My Vision of a Young Country* (Fourth Estate, 1996)
Flynn, Paul	*Commons Knowledge* (Seren, 1997)
Dale, Iain	*As I Said to Denis – The Margaret Thatcher Book of Quotations* (Robson Books, 1997)
Duncan, Alan	*Beware Blair!* (Conservative Central Office, 1997)
Farman, John	*The Very Bloody History of Britain Part 2* (Red Fox Books, 1997)
Gould, Bryan	*Goodbye to All That* (Macmillan, 1995)
Hoggart, Simon	*House of Correction* (Robson Books, 1995)
Layard, Richard	*What Labour Can Do* (Warner, 1997)
McSmith, Andy	*Faces of Labour* (Verso, 1996)
Norris, Steven	*Changing Trains* (Hutchinson, 1996)
Parris, Matthew	*Scorn* (Hamish Hamilton, 1995)
——	*I Couldn't Possibly Comment* (Robson Books, 1997)
Rentoul, John	*Tony Blair* (Warner, 1996)

Richards, Steve

Preparing for Power (New Statesman Books, 1997)

Sopel, Jon

Tony Blair – The Modernizer (Michael Joseph, 1995)

Willetts, David

Blair's Gurus (Centre for Policy Studies, 1996)

Williams, John

Victory – With Tony Blair on the Road to a Landslide (Buchman Publishing, 1997)

Wright, Tony

Socialisms Old and New (Routledge, 1996)